The Pubs of Monmouth, Chepstow & the Wye Valley

The Pubs of Monmouth, Chepstow & the Wye Valley

by

Heather Hurley

Logaston Press

LOGASTON PRESS
Little Logaston, Logaston,
Woonton, Almeley, Herefordshire HR3 6QH

First published by Logaston Press 2007
Copyright © Heather Hurley, 2007

ISBN 978 1904396 87 1

Set in Times New Roman by Logaston Press
and printed in Great Britain by
Bell and Bain Ltd., Glasgow

This book is dedicated to
Jon Hurley
for his continued support in seeking
the past and present pubs, inns and taverns

Sources of Illustrations

t – top; b – bottom; l – left; r – right; m – middle
References to collections are shown in brackets

Nelson Museum, Monmouth
12, 37 t & b, 45 t & b, 49 t & b, 51 t, 52 b, 60, 66, 69 b, 75 l, 81 t, 95, 96 b, 108 t, 109 t

Gwent Record Office
35, 48, 94 b (D10/1 292), 76, 96 t, 112,114 t, 117, 121 t, 131, 148, 160, 162, 163 t, 169, 186 t, 230 t (Misc. Mss. 406), 78 (Misc. Mss. 1786.1), 142 (D398/13.2), 172 (D412 81)

Gloucester Record Office
23, 120 t (D637/11/5/B2), 54 (D637/1/51)

Chepstow Library
18, 186 t, 201, 209, 228b, 234 b

Birmingham Museum and Art Gallery
33

Keith Kissack
34, 36, 67 t, 69 t, 75 r, 82 t, 89 b, 94 t, 97, 101 t, 108 b

Gill Howard-Jones
128 t, 129 r, 130 b, 136, 137, 138 m & b, 139, 189, 192 t, 204, 205 t, 229 b

Hereford Library
67 b

Neill Todd
98 b

Frank Bennett
106 t

Wye Valley Hotel
156, 167, 186 b

Chepstow Museum
228 t, 234 t

All other illustrations are from the author's collections or from the Logaston Press archives.

Contents

Acknowledgements

This is the author's third volume in the Logaston Press series on the social history of pubs. The *Pubs of Monmouth, Chepstow and the Wye Valley* complements the earlier *Pubs of Ross and South Herefordshire* and the *Pubs of the Royal Forest of Dean* to complete the course of the River Wye from Hereford to its mouth at Chepstow. The preparation of this work would not have been possible without the help and co-operation of many people who have provided information and illustrations. Thanks to Alwyn Nixon, Andrew Helme, Anne Rainsbury, Christine Thomas, Frank Bennett, Gill Howard-Jones, John Eisel, Jon Hurley, Katy Shoesmith, Keith Kissack, Sue Miles and my publishers Andy Johnson and Ron Shoesmith of Logaston Press.

Thanks are extended to the friendly and helpful staff at Monmouth Museum where information was readily available from maps, records, newspapers and local history books. Most documentary sources were researched at Gwent Record Office where whole days were spent because of the distance to travel. Other material was gathered from Monmouth Library, Chepstow Museum and an excellent Local Studies section at Chepstow Library where early newspapers were available on microfilm. A few gaps were filled from directories held at Hereford City Library, sale particulars at Gloucester Record Office and information from websites of individual pubs.

The sources of the illustrations used in this book are listed separately. Others are from the author's or publisher's collections.

Introduction

Writing the introduction to a book is the final and most difficult task to undertake after spending nearly three years researching, investigating and writing the history of roadside and riverside inns, old taverns, public houses and modest beer and cider houses in the delightful Wye Valley from Dixton lying north-east of Monmouth, to the Bulwark south of Chepstow.

Previously unknown back lanes and alleyways in the market towns of Monmouth and Chepstow have been investigated, and the remoter and wilder areas of the lower Wye have been explored in tracking down the sites of former licensed premises. These discoveries combined with information gleaned from documentary sources at museums, libraries and record offices has provided the history of the past and present pubs of the lower Wye Valley.

The sequence of chapters have been arranged to follow the Wye downstream from Monmouth to Chepstow via such notable places as Llandogo, Tintern and Trelleck. The two market towns have been divided into four sections according to their street plan, network of roads and riverside site. With its past navigation and famous Wye Tour, the river plays an important role and provides a fascinating link between the towns and villages where wharves were once commonplace, and where coaching inns catered for the early tourists.

The first two chapters cover the origin and development of inns, taverns and public houses, and the effects of varying legislation throughout the centuries. The procedure and history of cider making, brewing and malting are outlined, although untangling the early breweries at Redbrook presented a challenge. The expansion of the wine and spirit trade is covered from medieval times when Chepstow began to benefit from this important import from France.

Pubs have been altered and changed, opened and closed, built and rebuilt through the ages, and have served as social and business centres when there were few alternatives. Many were used as magistrates' courts, auction rooms and meeting places for friendly societies. In the 21st century pubs are used for quiz nights, dart matches, and venues for live music and watching sport on television, but their main use is for eating and drinking with family and friends. Pubs are now closing at an alarming rate, so use them instead of losing them, and the traditional pub will flourish.

Heather Hurley, Hoarwithy, August 2007.

THE LOWER WYE.
(MONMOUTH TO CHEPSTOW.)

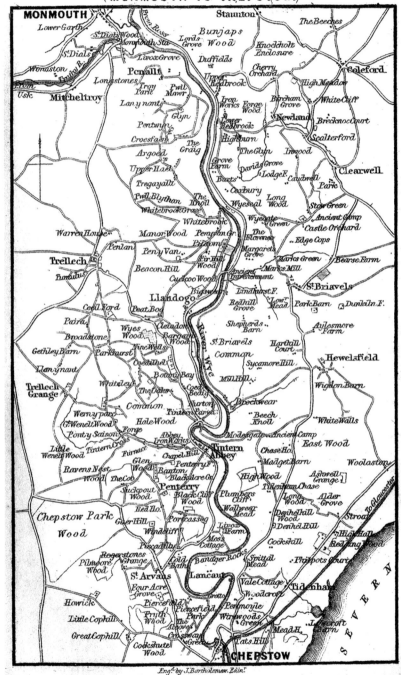

Engᵈ by J. Bartholomew, Edinᵇ

CHAPTER ONE

Inns, Taverns & Beer-houses

Only a few centuries ago the inn played many parts in the social economy
of this country. In a more primitive state of society, when public buildings
other than those devoted to ecclesiastical or military purposes were few and
far between, the inn as a place of resort, as a common meeting ground open
to the community at large, was used for a variety of public purposes.

(Frederick Hackwood 1904)

Ever since man realised that fermented grain, fruit and honey produced alcoholic beverages, communal drinking places were established in settlements and along the highways. In the Bronze Age mead was made from hemp and honey, and from fermented lime and honey flavoured with meadowsweet. It is thought that a strong cocktail was produced from hemp and cannabis mixed with alcohol. In the Iron Age a brew was made from emmer wheat, a type of cider from crab apples, and wine was imported from the Roman world in amphoræ – two-handled storage jars.

Monmouth and the lower Wye Valley enjoys a long history from prehistoric times with the river playing an important role in communication and trade. Iron Age hill forts have been identified including those at Buckholt, north of Monmouth; Gaer Hill, in Trellech parish; and Piercefield, north of Chepstow. At these settlements the inhabitants would have eaten a diet of wheat and barley and drunk a type of beer made from grain. This concoction was probably drunk communally during festivals, whilst during the Roman period a drink made from barley was often drunk instead of wine, although a Greek physician wrote 'it produces headaches, is a compound of bad juices, and does harm to the muscles'. At Monmouth, called *Blestium* by the Romans, on the junction of roads from *Ariconium*, Gloucester, Chepstow and Caerwent, the settlement probably would have provided accommodation and stabling in a *mansio*, a guesthouse for travellers.

It is understood that the area around Chepstow was well populated during the Roman period, although most of Monmouthshire must have been dominated by the large Roman town at Caerwent. Recent excavations at Chepstow have revealed enough evidence to confirm Roman occupation, and probably amongst the finds were fragments of amphoræ. These were usually associated with olive oil and apparently not wine, but it is known that the Romans poured a layer of olive oil on top of their wine containers to seal them. Throughout the Roman Empire a staple drink was produced by brewing and fermenting the fruit of vines and adding honey and spices.

As the Romans traversed the countryside between settlements, along the roads and over the river crossings, the predecessors of inns were established for the benefit of travellers and traders, both for rest and refreshment. These places would have been indicated by the earliest known sign of a bush, as explained by John Burke:

> The bush of ivy or vine leaves outside a Roman tavern might have been necessary until the place established its reputation, but once that was secure the drinking public knew where the best vintages were to be had [hence] a good wine needs no bush.

The break up of the Roman Empire in England and Wales took place following the withdrawal of the Roman troops shortly after 410 A.D. During the Dark Ages (between 784 and 796) King Offa constructed his great dyke marking the boundary between Wales and England. It closely followed the Wye between Chepstow and Monmouth before crossing the river to continue on its western side. Frederick Hackwood in his *Inns, Ales and Drinking Customs* of 1904 wrote:

> Our Saxon forefathers were notoriously addicted to the use of ale and mead, and regarded drunkenness as rather honourable than otherwise; for the man who could withstand the intoxicating effects of strong drink longest was the most admired and the one most respected among them.

Many churches in the lower Wye Valley were founded during this period when, according to Hackwood, 'there were three kinds of establishment open to the public, the Ale-house, the Wine-house and the Inn'.

The Normans left a lasting and dramatic legacy – castles, priories, churches

A 14th-century inn

2

and abbeys at Monmouth, Tintern and Chepstow, the remains of which are so admired today. At the priories of Monmouth and Chepstow, and at Tintern Abbey, refuge and lodgings would have been available. When Archbishop Baldwin and Gerald made their journey through the Welsh borders in 1188 the single meal of the day was served with 'unhopped ale or cider'. Otherwise travellers stayed in inns that offered little comfort – a bed in a shared room, a meal of meat, a little bread and some beer. Hackwood also adds:

> The beds ... could not be constdered dear at a penny a head in London, and sometimes less in the country, servants being generally charged at half these rates. The modern traveller might think them dear at any price when it is stated that they were invariably overrun with fleas, bugs and other vermin.
>
> In addition to the inns where wayfarers slept at nights there were lesser establishments along the highway, and nearly always at the roads crossings – mere calling-places known as ale-houses. These could always be seen a long way off if the weary traveller but raised his eyes to look ahead for the one common sign which distinguished them all. From above the front door of every ale-house projected a long, horizontal pole, on the top of which was a thick bush. In the towns it became necessary to regulate the length and height of these signs, as not infrequently they were affixed so low as to endanger the heads of horsemen riding along the narrow thoroughfares of a crowded city. An act of 1375 restricted them to a minimum of 7 feet above the public road.

There was a growth in population after the Norman Conquest. This led to various measures being taken, both to limit the numbers of drinking houses and to protect the customer. One of the provisions of *Magna Carta* in 1215 was that there were to be standard measures for wine, ale and corn. This was followed with the *Assize of Bread and Ale* in 1266, which ensured the retail price of ale was fixed to the price of grain.

During the 13th century there was a gradual increase in the sale of wine, and a separation came into being between taverns, which sold both ale and wine, and alehouses, which sold ale only. In addition to these there were the wayside inns or hostels that provided accommodation for travellers as well as food and drink. At

The bush often hung out some distance across the road

that time brewers at Monmouth paid a levy of 1 *ob* 'on every vat and lead cooling trough for brewing', and at Chepstow there was a proportionary tax on ale brewed in the borough.

Monastic establishments had offered rest and refreshment to travellers, but once the influence of the church began to wane, and merchants started to travel, inns and alehouses became a common feature in the countryside, at crossroads, river crossings and in the urban communities. Although there had been previous attempt at curtailing the number of drinking houses, the first formal licensing law came at the end of the 15th

*A 14th-century tavern with
a cellar underneath for storage*

century. This empowered Justices of the Peace to obtain sureties for good behaviour from the landlords and, if necessary, to close alehouses. Some 50 years later the justices obtained the power, which they still retain, to both license and suppress alehouses – hence 'licensed premises'.

Legislation continued and 1553 saw an Act of Parliament that curtailed the number of 'taverns' and thus limited the sale of wine. Indeed, the Act also prohibited the sale of French wines. The limits on taverns provide an indication of the size and importance of the towns at that time – London was allowed 40; York, nine; and Bristol, six. Gloucester was limited to four, the same as Exeter, Chester, Norwich and Hull. This did not mean that the population of the country was being deprived of places in which to drink – there were approximately 44 alehouses for every tavern in the latter part of the 16th century! This was equivalent to more than one drinking establishment for every 200 persons, a far higher ratio than exists today. These early alehouses were probably little different to the timber-framed and thatched houses that surrounded them. The larger ones would have had sheds at the rear where brewing was carried out and possibly cellars to protect their brew from temperature variations.

Taverns, being of a higher status, were probably of a superior construction. This may well be the reason why the more important towns and cities in the country tend to be well endowed with substantial stone cellars of a late medieval date. They were obviously designed for public use and usually had well-constructed vaulted roofs and entries leading directly from the streets.

During the settled years of Elizabeth's reign the inn first enters its great days in the market towns, along the highways between the towns and trading centres and at important sites and river crossings to cater for

A 16th-century brewer

travellers. The inns and taverns were also meeting and trading places as described by Andre Simon:

> In all the better-class taverns there were a number of private rooms either on the street level or on the first floor; sometimes even on the second floor. The regular patrons of each tavern had the privilege of meeting in one or other of those private rooms. There they could discuss in private, politics and religion, if so was their wish, and that at a time when political and religious opinions were not only extreme but highly dangerous. In the privacy of the room that was theirs for the evening, they could argue to their heart's content, drink toasts that were not loyal, tell tales that would not bear repeating, and generally enjoy each other's company.

There is little documentary evidence of inns in the lower Wye Valley during the 16th century, but as travel and transportation began to increase some alehouses must have existed which later blossomed into coaching inns at a later date. Keith Kissack, in his book on Monmouth, wrote:

> By 1552 all innkeepers had to be licensed. Even so, vast quantities of ale were consumed, encouraged by the practice of many farmers paying their labourers in ale. As a result the Privy Council, through the Council in the Marches, sent a directive to Monmouthshire complaining of the continuing surfeit of alehouses ... Few attempts by the Elizabethans to restrict drinking were successful; one that was doomed from the start was the decree that tippling in any alehouse should not last for more than one hour.

16   99

Whereas by the Laws and Statutes of This Realm

NOTICE

IS HEREBY GIVEN TO ALL

INN KEEPERS, ALEHOUSE KEEPERS, SUTLERS, VICTUALLERS

and other Retailers of

ALE and BEER

AND EVERY OTHER PERSON or PERSONS KEEPING A PUBLIC HOUSE
IN ANY
CITY, TOWN CORPORATE, BOROUGH, MARKET TOWN, VILLAGE, HAMLET, PARISH,
PART or PLACE IN THE *Kingdom of England*

That, as from the **24**th *day of* **JUNE, 1700**

THEY SHALL BE REQUIRED TO RETAIL and SELL THEIR ALE & BEER

by the **FULL ALE QUART** or **PINT**

According to the Laid Standard

IN VESSELS DULY MARKED *with* **W.R** *and* **CROWN**

be they made of

WOOD, GLASS, HORN, LEATHER or **PEWTER** *etc.*

Any Person Retailing Ale or Beer to a **TRAVELLER** *or* **WAYFARER** *in Vessels not
signed and marked as aforesaid will be liable to a* **PENALTY** *not exceeding*

FORTY SHILLINGS

FOR EVERY SUCH OFFENCE

By Act of Parliament ~ at WESTMINSTER
In the Reign of Our Sovereign ~ WILLIAM III by the Grace of God, King,
Defender of the Faith &c

*By 1700 it became a legal requirement that vessels in which ale and beer
were served should be accurate and marked*

At the time of the Civil War, Monmouthshire had a higher proportion of Catholics than any county in England or Wales, but they were concentrated in the north and east of the county, and Chepstow 'had not a single convicted recusant under Elizabeth or the Stuarts' and was a busy port with links to puritan Gloucester and Bristol. The stores in the castle captured by the Parliamentarians in 1645 included ' 4,000 weight each of cheese and biscuits, 30 barrels of salt, three hogsheads of metheglin (mead) and four of beer and ale' plus other stocks of food, and barrels of gunpowder which had been collected by Sir John Wintour.

Various attempts were made during the Civil War to levy duty on both the manufacture and the sale of beer and ale – attempts which were consolidated following that war and still apply to this day. This was when beer was brewed in three different qualities: strong, table, and small, and each variety attracted a different rate of duty. It was not until the late 19th century that the duty levied became based on the original gravity of the beer. The specific gravity (density) of the liquor before fermentation gives an indication of the amount of sugars present and therefore the likely alcoholic content of the final brew. Prior to the use of a hydrometer other methods were used to judge the strength of the beer, one of which was for the examining officer to don a pair of leather breeches, pour some of the beer to be tested upon a stone step and then sit on it. If, at the end of a specified time, he found that he was stuck to the step, the the beer was deemed to be strong!

After the turmoil of the Civil War a revolution in road travel began, so town and wayside inns played a more important role, as Richardson describes:

A mid-18th-century brewhouse

The large houses flourished on the influx of new custom and on their new-found importance as stages in a regular coaching system; and the amenities they offered must have been a substantial comfort to the shaken passenger deposited there after an arduous day's journeying. From the mass of contemporary evidence available, it would seem that landlords were now genuinely eager to do their best for travellers. The rooms were well furnished at the larger inns, which catered for regular as well as chance custom, the supply of food and drink was generous, the stables were roomy, and the ostlers, waiters and serving-maids generally civil and obliging.

Inn signs had developed from the Middle Ages when the tavern, inn and alehouse needed to identify themselves in a visual manner to a population that was mainly illiterate. The earlier signs chosen usually represented an association with a religious house, a local family, trade, or place. The sign depicting a Crown often indicated an establishment dating from the Restoration and the King's Head expressed loyalty to the reigning monarch. The Bear appears to have pre-dated these names and together with the Bell were popular signs in the Wye Valley, followed by the later Sloop, Ship, Boat, and Bridge, all connected with the Wye and its navigation.

In the 18th century more pack horses, cumbersome wagons, traders' carts, carriages and droves of livestock were using the inadequate and narrow roads as described by Heath: 'a barbarous holloway, six feet below the surface of the ground, thro' which the traveller had to wade, bemired in clay, till he gained the summit of this tedious eminence at Penalt common'. He also wrote 'Before the formation of the turnpike roads in this county, which took place in the year 1755, the general method of travelling to and from London and South Wales, was by common stage wagon'. The turnpike system was adopted nationwide to improve the roads with trusts set up at various dates including Chepstow in 1758, but the Wye Valley road between the two towns was not constructed until after the Road Act of 1824.

With the introduction of mail and coach routes to London, Bristol, Hereford and South Wales, roadside alehouses developed into coaching inns and post houses offering rest and refreshment to the weary traveller. The stable-yards presented a busy scene, with impatient horses waiting to be harnessed, saddled, watered or stabled, and coaches with passengers arriving and departing. Neighbouring activities included a smithy to replace loose or cast shoes, a wheelwright to repair coach wheels, wagon loads of hay and fodder being delivered, gallons of water being manually pumped and piles of manure heaped onto a dung pit.

A similar busy scene would have been seen along the riverside especially at Monmouth and Chepstow where the navigation along the Wye to Hereford and Bristol was an important industry. In 1792 Coxe recorded that 2,800 tons

Published for Bettering the Condition and Increasing the Comforts of the POOR.

CAUTION

To Alehouse Keepers, & their Guests.

It is better that Offences against the Laws should be Prevented, *than that Offenders should be* Punished.

THE PROPER USE OF INNS, &c.

THE proper use of Inns and Alehouses, is to furnish Refreshment and Lodging to Travellers, upon a reasonable profit; to accommodate persons meeting on *necessary* business; Soldiers in his Majesty's service; and some whose occupations require a frequent change of residence, or who cannot provide themselves with meat and drink in a more convenient manner.

The neighbouring Justices of the Peace have the Power of granting a License for keeping a Publick House, and they have the like Power of refusing to grant a License, without giving any reason whatever for such refusal, which is entirely at their discretion; it is therefore the Interest as well as the Duty of an Alehouse keeper to take care, that he conduct himself and his House in a becoming manner, lest he forfeit the good opinion of the Justices and be deprived of his License.

A principal duty of an Alehouse keeper is to prevent Artificers and Labourers from drinking more than for their necessary Refreshment; and not to allow them to lose their time and spend their money to the injury of themselves and their families: therefore, almost all debts (commonly called Ale Scores) are incurred in an improper manner; and are such, as the lawful means (if any) of recovering such debts would often discover bad conduct in the Alehouse keeper, and hazard the loss of his License.

The Law protects the Alehouse keeper from losses, by giving him the power of detaining the Person of any Guest who refuses to pay the reasonable charges for the meat and drink which have been furnished him: Debts are seldom incurred by Travellers, who are generally Strangers, and when they are incurred by Artificers and Labourers, great blame will attach to the Alehouse keeper from the manner in which such Ale Scores must have been contracted.

An Alehouse keeper is liable to heavy penalties for allowing Tippling, Drunkenness, or disorderly behaviour in his House, extending to the Forfeiture of his Recognizance, and that of his Surety or Bondsman, and the loss of his License.

The Guests who are guilty of Tippling, Drunkenness, and disorderly Behaviour are also liable to heavy penalties; and Artificers and Labourers who waste their time and their money at Publick Houses, ought to consider that although they may avoid punishment from the forbearance with which the Laws are executed, yet their Wives and their Families cannot escape from the miseries of Poverty, the certain consequence of their Husband's misconduct; and that the wholesome restraint which the Law lays upon a man in this respect, gives the best assurance of protection to his Family and to Himself, when it forbids him to waste his time and his money in a Publick House, and disturb the peace of others by his intemperance and bad example.

To   *Alehouse keeper.*

You are desired to have this Paper pasted up in your Kitchen, or some other usual place where your Guests take their Refreshment.

SIGNED

A caution to alehouse keepers (mid-19th century)

The 19th-century apprentice had to forswear all drinking-houses!

of goods, which included grain, timber, coal, mill-stones, paper, and cider, were shipped from Chepstow where there was a flourishing trade in wine. A variety of goods including bark, stone and coal were delivered to the wharves at Monmouth to be conveyed by barges to Ross and Hereford, and downstream to Llandogo, Brockweir, Tintern and Chepstow. So there would have been a demand for alcoholic beverages from the bargees and traders at the local beer houses and riverside pubs.

The Hon. John Byng during his tour of South Wales in 1781 left a lasting account of inns at Monmouth and Chepstow. He was not impressed with the **Beaufort Arms** at Monmouth 'now sitting in a mean room at this bad inn; which may be the best here. The stables are new and good, that's a comfort; for if my horse does not fare and sleep well, why there wou'd be an end of my travell'. He sheltered from a storm at a public house in Trellech and discussed goats and the Welsh language with the landlord, and at Tintern he 'alighted at the Beaufort Arms (the sign of all this country)'. At Chepstow he stayed at the **Three Cranes**, which he discovered was owned by the same person as the **Beaufort Arms** on the opposite side of the square. In an old South Wales pub, not far from Monmouth, the *Rules of the Inn* dating from the late 18th century hang in the bar (see opposite).

In the 1780s the *Gloucester Journal* advertised that: 'John Philpotts and Co. Proprietors of the Original London and Gloucester Post-Coaches' were continuing their service to south-west Ireland in 'an elegant Post-Coach, (Carrying four persons only, inside)'. The London coach went through several towns including Gloucester and Chepstow to Haverfordwest 'where three well-manned Packets' conveyed passengers and parcels to Waterford for the price of £1 17s., but outside passengers were half the cost.

A vivid impression of 18th-century travellers arriving at an inn is described by Richardson:

The tired traveller arriving at one of the large solid inns of the later eighteenth century would generally have been justified in expecting the highest degee of 'comfort and elegance'. If the coach was timed to stop for half-an-hour to change horses and enable the passengers to dine, the waiters woulld be standing at the door in readiness to assist him with his hat, shawl and coat. The landlord and landlady would be waiting in the hall, where there would be a good display of cold meats, game pies, cheeses and pastries on view in a special glazed cupboard. The coffee room or dining parlour would reveal an immense central table, round or rectangular, laid in readiness for the meal, with good plated cutlery and spotless table linen. Some inns could boast a special dining room for coach passengers, while the upstairs bedrooms, each with its curtained four-poster and good plain furniture, often of mahogany, including a mirror, a washing-table and a wig-stand, were still generally known by individual names such as the Moon, Star, Crescent, or Paragon.

Although there was a duty on beer, spirits were exempt and towards the end of the 17th century, and well into the 18th, there was what Monckton, in his *History of the English Public House*, described as 'one of the biggest orgies of over-indulgence our island history has ever seen'. Every small alehouse in the country was in a position to sell cheap brandy and, in partic-ular, gin. The result was that consumption of spirits, sold in taverns, inns, alehouses, brandy-shops, dram-shops, and by street hawkers, increased from half-a-million gallons in 1684 to over 8 million gallons in 1743 – an increase of well over one gallon per person per year! This was the 'Gin Era', a period of drunkenness, misery and total wretchedness so well depicted by Hogarth. The various 'Gin Acts' that followed, together with increased duties and a strengthening of the powers of the Justices, rapidly changed this trend, but it was not until 1751 that the sale of spirits was successfully brought under the

---

RULES OF THE INN
No Thieves, Fakirs, Rogues or Tinkers
No Skulking Loafers or Flea-Bitten Tramps
No Slap an Tickle o' the Wenches
No Banging o' Tankards on the Tables
No Dogs allowed in the Kitchen
No Cockfighting

Flintlocks, Cudgels, Daggers and Swords
to be handed to the Innkeeper
for safe-keeping

Bed for the Night – 1 Shilling
Stabling for the Horse – 4 pence

OLD WYE COACH·
MAY—FROM MONMOUTH.
8, Monday ....7 morning.... 2¼ afternoon
9, Tuesday .... 2½ afternoon
10, Wednesday .... 2⅖ afternoon
11, Thursday .... 2¼ afternoon
12, Friday .... 8¼ morning
13, Saturday ..8½ morning.... 2⅖ afternoon
MAY—FROM CHEPSTOW.
8, Monday ....10 morning
9, Tuesday ....10½ morning
10, Wednesday..............11 morning
11, Thursday..11½ morning ....5 afternoon
12, Friday ....2½ afternoon
13, Saturday ....12½ morning

The May 1865 coach service between
Monmouth and Chepstow

control of the Justices with licences issued to those already possessing an alehouse licence, and by 1758 excise duty was paid on less than two million gallons per year.

From the end of the 18th century and into the early years of the next, came the great coaching era. Apart from the traditional stage-coachmen, fashionable men drove their own lavish vehicles, drawn by quality horses. A breakfast was often served to private parties in a separate parlour of the inn, such as that taken by Lord Nelson and his companions at Ross in 1802, and at the Kymin Pavilion overlooking the Wye and the town of Monmouth. During the early 19th century Charles Heath, bookseller and antiquarian from Monmouth, wrote in detail about Lord Nelson's visits in his *Excursion Down the Wye,* but this volume contains much more interesting material of Heath's own excursions during the early 19th century. At Lea 'is a respectable Inn, should the traveller be disposed to take advantage of its hospitality'. He found the inn a 'House fitted up in the most elegant manner, and visitors will meet with every accommodation, from its present occupier'. Travelling from Chepstow to St. Briavels, Heath noted a 'Public House' where 'the visitor will have his horse taken care of, while he notices the scenes on the Wye', and at St. Briavels he observed 'The Castle is now a public house', and added 'the traveller may pass a little time very pleasantly, in surveying these ruins, with the attendant scenery, here noticed; and, being half-way between Chepstow and Monmouth, in the village will meet with a clean room, and his horses taken care of, at either of the two public houses, which adjoin the side of the road'.

By the 19th century the Friendly Societies in Monmouth and Chepstow were well established. The earliest ones were founded during the late 18th century to provide a form of insurance for the less wealthy against sickness, disability and old age by means of a weekly subscription. They were closely associated with public houses, and many were called the *Hearts*

12

DRUNKARD'S CATECHISM

1. Q. What is your name?
   A. Drunken sot.
2. Q. Who gave you that name?
   A. As drink is my idol, Landlords and their wives get all my money; they gave me that name in one of my drunken sprees, wherein I was made a member of strife, a child of want, and an inheritor of a bundle of rage.
3. Q. What did your Landlords and Landladies promise for you?
   A. They did promise and vow three things in my name; first, that I should renounce the comforts of my own fireside; second, starve my wife and hunger my children; third, walk in rags and tatters, with my shoe soles going flip flap, all the days of my life.
4. Q. Rehearse the articles of the belief.
   A. I believe in the existence of one Mr. Alcohol, the great head and chief of all manner of vice, the source of nine-tenths of all diseases; lastly, I not only believe, but am sure when my money is all gone and spent, the Landlord will stop the tap and turn me out.
5. Q. How many commandments have ye sots to keep?
   A. Ten.
6. Q. Which be they?
   A. The same which the Landlord and Landlady spoke in the bar, saying, We are thy master and mistress, who brought thee out of the paths of virtue, placed thee in the ways of vice, and set thy feet in the road which leadeth to New South Wales.
   I. Thou shalt use no other house but mine.
   II. Thou shalt not make for thyself any substitute for intoxicating drinks, such as tea, coffee, ginger pop, or lemonade; for I am a jealous man, wearing a coat that should be on thy back, eating thy children's bread, and pocketing the money which should make thee and the wife comfortable all the days of thy life.
   III. Thou shalt not use my house in vain.
   IV. Remember that thou eat but one meal on the Sabbath day, for six days hast thou been drinking, and nought else wouldst thou do; but the seventh is the sabbath day, and thou canst have no trust; therefore thou skulketh on the seventh day and abominates it.
   V. Thou shalt honour the Landlords and Landladies and Gin-shops with thy presence, that thy days may be few and miserable in the land wherein thou dwellest.
   VI. Thou shalt commit murder, by starving, and hungering, and beating thy wife and family.
   VII. Thou shalt commit self-destruction.
   VIII. Thou shalt sell thy wife and children's bread and rob thyself of all thy comforts.
   IX. Thou shalt bear false witness when thou speakest of the horrors, saying thou art in good health when thou art labouring under the barrel fever.
   X. Thou shalt covet all thy neighbour is possessed of, thou shalt covet his house, his land, his purse, his health, his wealth, and all that he has got, that thou mayest indulge in drinking, help the brewer to buy a new coach, a pair of fine horses, a new dray and a fine building, that he may live in idleness all his days: likewise to enable the Landlord to purchase a new sign to put over his door, with 'Licensed to be drunk on the premises', written thereon.

An 1850s Temperance Society Tract based on the Ten Commandments

One of the Chepstow Friendly Societies advertising its annual dinner in 1898

of *Oak*, the *Order of Foresters* and the *Order of Buffaloes*, while others took their name from the meeting place or from a trade, one of the most original being the *Chepstow Free Gardeners' Friendly Society* of 1847.

The 19th century saw the rise of the Temperance Movement, designed to encourage less drunkenness, for many criminal cases were found to be drink related. The movement started in England around 1820, from American influences, and in 1840 the *Monmouth Total Abstinence Society* held their first meeting, followed by the formation of the *Band of Hope* at Chepstow. The influence of the Temperance Movement led to a few licensed premises being closed or converted into temperance hotels in the 1880s and 1890s. In 1881 the members of the movement welcomed the *Sunday Closure Act* which was originally introduced throughout Wales and in parts lasted until 1961.

Old **C Y D E R** for **Ever!**

A 1765 woodcut celebrating the repeal of the cider tax

Apart from earlier attempts to regulate the marking of drinking vessels to show the capacity, it was during the 19th century that most of the legislation that affects the present-day consumption and sale of alcoholic drink was enacted. The Alehouse Act of 1828 meant that the licensee no longer had to find sureties for his behaviour. However, he was bound to use the legal, stamped measures, not to adulterate his drinks, and not to permit drunkenness on his premises. The Beerhouse Acts of 1830, 1834 and 1840 followed – the first allowed premises to open for the sale of beer, but not spirits, on

An Act to prohibit the Sale of Intoxicating Liquors on Sunday in Wales.

[27th August 1881.]

WHEREAS the provisions in force against the sale of fermented and distilled liquors during certain hours of Sunday have been found to be attended with great public benefits, and it is expedient and the people of Wales are desirous that in the principality of Wales those provisions be extended to the other hours of Sunday :

Be it therefore enacted by the Queen's most Excellent Majesty, by and with the advice and consent of the Lords Spiritual and Temporal, and Commons, in this present Parliament assembled, and by the authority of the same, as follows :

1. In the principality of Wales all premises in which intoxicating liquors are sold or exposed for sale by retail shall be closed during the whole of Sunday. *Premises where intoxicating liquors sold to be closed on Sundays in Wales.*

2. The Licensing Acts, 1872–1874, shall apply in the case of any premises closed under this Act as if they had been closed under those Acts. *Application of Licensing Acts. 35 & 36 Vict. c. 94. 37 & 38 Vict. c. 49.*

3. This Act shall commence and come into operation with respect to each division or place in Wales on the day next appointed for the holding of the general annual licensing meeting for that division or place. *Commencement of Act.*

4. Nothing in this Act contained shall preclude the sale at any time at a railway station of intoxicating liquors to persons arriving at or departing from such station by railway. *Sale of intoxicating liquors at railway stations.*

5. This Act may be cited as the Sunday Closing (Wales) Act, 1881. *Short title.*

The 1881 Welsh Sunday Closing Act

payment of a simple excise licence; the second differentiated between 'on' and 'off' licences and made 'on' licences more difficult to obtain; whilst the third ensured that licences were issued only to the occupier of the premises. Throughout the country as a whole there was a proliferation of beer-houses following the first Act, many in the country areas.

When the railways rapidly took over from coach travel and navigation on the Wye, many coaching and riverside inns closed due to lack of business, but changes in licensing laws led to the opening of small beer houses in towns and villages where the beer retailer often doubled as a plumber, mason, builder, tailor or some other trade in order to make a living. Even after the 1872 Licensing Act inns and ale houses were, in general, still allowed to open for some 20 hours each day.

After the Second World War there were several minor Acts, which culminated in the 1961 Act that provided for 'restaurant' and 'residential' licences. It also gave the customers grace – the ten minutes of 'drinking-up time'. A late 20th-century Act restored the situation to more or less what it had been at the beginning of the century by allowing inns to stay open throughout the day if they so wished, most commonly any times between 11a.m. and 11p.m., with a somewhat shorter 'window of opportunity' on Sundays. A new millennium has brought new thought and restrictions have been further reduced leading to the availability of 24-hour opening once again.

Since the Licensing Laws of 2005 came into force, *The Spectator* in November 2006 reported that:

Britain's drinking habits have hardly changed since 24-hour licensing laws came into effect a year ago, new research has found; Government statistics show that 3,000 premises now have licenses to sell booze round the clock, but one in five closes by 11 pm, half by midnight and four-fifths by 1 am. Of the premises permitted to serve 24 hours, 20 per cent are pubs, bars and clubs, 20 per cent convenience stores, a quarter supermarkets and 35 per cent others, including hotels.

CHAPTER TWO

Cider Makers, Brewers & Wine Merchants

When there was a limited range of drinks, cider, perry and mead were very popular beverages in the Wye Valley, where all the ingredients were readily available. Cider was a medieval drink and Kissack records the Monmouth accounts showing that 60 gallons were sold in 1256 for 2 shillings. In the 17th century, cider was renowned for its medicinal powers as described by John Evelyn: 'Generally all strong and pleasant cider excites and cleanses the Stomach, strengthens Digestion, and infallibly frees the Kidnies and Bladder from breeding the Gravel Stone'. Defoe in 1726 followed this with:

so very good, so fine and so cheap ... great quantities of this are sent to London, even by land carriage tho' so very remote, which is an evidence of the goodness of it beyond contradiction.

A 17th-century recipe for making 'Mead of the best sort' was to:

Take twelve gallons of water and slip in the whites of six eggs; mix them well with the water and twenty pounds of good honey; let the liquor boil an hour, and when boiled add cinnamon, ginger, cloves, mace, and a little rosemary; as soon as it is cold put a spoonful of yeast to it, and turn it up, keeping the vessel filled as it works; when it has done working, stop up close, and when fine bottle it for use.

Cider was conveyed by barge to Monmouth and Chepstow from Herefordshire which was famed for its cider and perry, but in 1786 Edward Davies, the Chepstow poet, wrote:

No better cider does the world supply
Than grows along thy borders, gentle Wye.
Delicious, strong and exquisitely fine,
With all the friendly properties of wine.

17

A 1757 engraving of cider making

Heath in 1804 noted the 'rich orcharding and fruit trees, producing the best kinds of cider and perry' along the banks of the Wye, and at Penalt most farms and several cottages had cider presses to make cider, which was a powerful brew.

Cider was sometimes produced as a cash crop, but was usually used by the farmer's family and his labourers. In the 19th century the custom of paying labourers partly in cider and perry increased. Cider is made from bitter-sweet apples, which are richer in sugar but rather unpleasant to the taste as they contain a lot of tannin. After crushing the apples and pressing to extract the juice, farm cider was produced without the addition of cultural yeast, as the fermentation relied upon the natural yeasts in the apples to produce a still, cloudy, acidic, invigorating and thirst-quenching drink. This was much appreciated during the heat of the next summer when the farmer would provide bread, cheese, and cider for those helping with hay-making, a practice that continued well into the 20th century.

In 1595 there was a cider mill in Welsh Street, Chepstow, and in 1633 a 'messuage, barn, sider mill and all other messuages' at Rockfield. The Hon. John Byng recorded that 'bread, beer, cyder, and commonly salmon, may be had at the Beaufort Arms, Tintern' and during the mid 19th century there was

An 1897 advertisement for Chepstow cider

a 'cider house' and a 'Cyder Millhouse' in Monnow Street, with John Howells trading in cider at Cinderhill in Monmouth. In 1871 William Pugh was listed as a cider maker at Tintern, where the **Anchor** in 1899 had a 'Cyder Mill and

Cellar, with Stores over' about the same time that Enoch Evans was cider making at Wonastow.

During the 20th century cider was produced in many parts of the country on a more commercial basis, but in Monmouthshire there is little evidence to suggest that this happened. Since then the taste for cider and perry has become more popular according to the *Cider Pub Guide to South Wales*. It lists **Orchards Farmhouse** from Brockweir, cider served at the **Lion** at Trellech, the **Stonemill** at Rockfield, the **Moon and Sixpence** at Tintern, the Boat at Penalt and the **Wye Valley Hotel** at Tintern where Blakeney Red Perry is also available.

With a long tradition of malting and brewing it appears that beer was the preferred drink in the Wye Valley, as was the case in the Forest of Dean. From Offa's time 'Welsh' Ale was a sweet ale more like barley wine, which was regarded as 'glutinous, heady and soporific'. A land rent paid to the church of Worcester at Offa's time included 'three hogsheads of Welsh ale, sweetened with honey', which was then the commonest drink in Wales. At Chepstow in the early 14th century, brewers produced ale for which a prise – a proportionary tax – had to be paid, and at Monmouth brewers were liable to the custom of Castle Couches – a toll of 17 gallons for every brew – to the king.

In the *Inns and Friendly Societies of Monmouth* by Davies and Kissack, an inventory of a brewhouse in Monnow Street is described as follows; 'two furnaces, two great vats, two watering tubs, two churns, one hairsieve, two cowls, fourteen Betchings and two Bonnys'. Most beer was brewed on the premises of inns and ale houses or in the brewhouse of a country house, but the malt was supplied from a growing number of maltsters recorded from the 17th century at Monmouth, Redbrook, Tintern and Chepstow. Water was essential for brewing and according to Heath in 1804 it was obtained as follows:

> The soft water used for washing or brewing purposes, is sold in casks, which the housekeepers purchase of people employed in hauling it, with a one-horse team, from the Wye, – at a rate of 6d. the half hogshead.

The 1811 *Book of Trades* states:

THE BREWER

The art of brewing is of very high antiquity, but in no country has it been carried to greater perfection than in our own. The different counties are, many of them, celebrated for their peculiar ales, and London porter is famous in almost all parts of the civilized world. Different as these several sorts of liquor are, they are nevertheless composed of the same materials variously prepared.

MONMOUTH BREWERY

WALTER ALABASTER,
ALE *and* PORTER BREWER,
Wine and Spirit Merchant,

Invites the attention of the Public to his

PALE, MILD, & STRONG ALES,

Which are unsurpassed for Purity, Delicacy of Flavour, and Fine Tonic Properties.

THE 'BEAUFORT' PALE ALE,

At 1s. 4d. per Gallon; and Beaufort Bitter Ale, at 1s. per Gallon;

BREWED ESPECIALLY FOR PRIVATE FAMILIES, in Casks of 9, 18, 36, or 54 Gallons.

Also Porter and Extra Stout, at 1s. 2d. and 1s. 5d. per Gallon,

Worcester Street, MONMOUTH.

*Walter Alabaster was the Brewer and Wine and Spirit Merchant
at the Brewery in Worcester Street*

During the 19th century larger and more commercial brewing enterprises were established, although at Chepstow documentation reveals that John Jones had established an independent brewhouse by 1733 which was probably the same 'brew house of Thomas Walters' mentioned in a lease of 1798. Despite the fourteen maltsters of the 1830s in Monmouth, which included George Tippins, it appears to have taken him at least 30 years before he established the Monmouth Steam Brewery Company in Inch Lane – about the same time that William Dugmore was brewing in St James Street.

In 1884 George Porter Tippins was listed as a maltster and corn merchant in St Mary's Street, and Walter Alabaster was the brewer and wine and spirit merchant at the Brewery, Worcester Street. In 1888 the Monmouth Brewery was brewing Pure Malt Beer and supplying 'Mild Beer at 10d. per Gal., Light Bitter Beer 1s. per Gal., Beaufort Pale Ale 1s. 2d. per Gal., Strong Stock Beer 1s. 6d. per Gal.' Alabaster was followed by Searle & Co. in 1895, but in 1905 the Monmouth Brewery Co. 'Family Ale and Porter Brewers' was under the Tippins name again. Harry Rowland was listed as the proprietor of the

The former Monmouth Brewery

brewery in 1910 and by 1924 had gone into partnership with Cossens an 'ale, stout and cider bottler, and wine and spirit merchant' in St. Mary's Street. It appears that two years later a representative from the Newport brewery called Lloyd & Yorath Ltd., registered in 1895, had replaced the Monmouth Brewery by one of their representatives in Monnow Street.

Some of the earliest breweries established in the Wye Valley were at Redbrook, a difficult place to research due to its being divided by country, county and parish boundaries in English Gloucestershire and Welsh Monmouthshire. A preliminary account of the Redbrook Brewery is in the *Pubs of the Royal Forest of Dean*, but further research has been carried out for this book. At least three breweries existed at Redbrook. One was established by Richard Sims in 1825, who placed the following advertisement in the *Monmouth Merlin* before retiring in 1835.

> [He] begs to thank his friends and the Public for the patronage he has experienced, and also to inform them he is succeeded by his brother, Edward Sims, who he is sure will do his utmost to offer a malt beverage of the choicest flavour. Edward Sims, late of the firm of John and Edward Sims, of the Stroudwater Brewery, having dissolved partnership with his brother on the 25th day of March last, begs to inform the public that he has taken the Redbrook Brewery.

The documentation is unclear, but it does appear that James Hall, already established as a maltster, brickmaker and wine merchant at Redbrook by 1830, acquired the Redbrook Upper Brewery a few years later. In 1840 three brewers were listed at Redbrook – James Hall, Wilmont Reynolds and

*An 1853 advertisement for the
Redbrook Upper Brewery*

Graterax & Dyke – with only two listed in 1849 – Charles Herbert and James Hall jun. Due to his father's death, a Chancery case and debts incurred by the brick trade, the brewery was 'To be Let or Sold' in 1855 with its 'commodious Malthouse, compact three-quarter Brewery' and 'constant supply of excellent water'. Two years later the property was still up for sale, and the particulars offered the buyer:

a desirable opportunity for making a mere investment, or for enabling a purchaser to carry on the extensive Malting and Brewery business long connected with the property.

*Change of ownership at
the Redbrook Brewery in 1856*

James Hall of the Redbrook Upper Brewery placed a notice in the *Monmouth Beacon* in 1853 thanking customers for their support. This was followed three years later with an announcement that Charles Herbert had sold the Redbrook Brewery to Thomas Burgham, and in 1859 the only brewer listed at Redbrook was Thomas Burgham & Son. The Burgham family ran and

DESIRABLE INVESTMENT.

REDBROOK,
NEAR MONMOUTH.

TO BE SOLD
BY AUCTION,

BY MR. WILLIAM COURT,

At the **BEAUFORT ARMS INN**, Monmouth,
On *WEDNESDAY, the 18th March*, 1857,
At Three o'clock in the Afternoon, (subject to Conditions of Sale,)

A FREEHOLD DWELLING
HOUSE

WITH THE MALTHOUSE, BREWERY,

Orchard and Garden, and about **10 Acres of rich land**, chiefly Orcharding, in full bearing, thereto adjoining and belonging, now in the occupation of Mr. James Hall.

The MALTHOUSE is large and convenient, and the BREWERY is very compact. The House and Premises are pleasantly situated, abundantly supplied with pure spring water, and offer a desirable opportunity for making a mere investment, or for enabling a purchaser to carry on the extensive Malting and Brewery business long connected with the property.

For further particulars apply to the *AUCTIONEER* ; or to Messrs. Jas. and J. ENDELL POWLES, Solicitors, Monmouth.

Sale of the Redbrook Brewery in 1857

extended the business, and supplied at least 22 licensed premises either owned or tied to the Redbrook Brewery. In 1923 Ind, Coope & Co. took over the business and in 1926 the brewery buildings were demolished. On the opposite bank of the Wye at Whitebrook the Kingstone Brewery opened in 2005, producing the Three Castles Brew amongst others.

At Rockfield James Williams, a wheelwright was brewing until his death in 1829, and at Trelleck brewing took place in a brewhouse that was erected between 1809 and 1833 on the site of a forge which was leased to William Williams in 1833 for £415. The property consisted of a dwelling house, garden, barn, brewhouse, stables, and granary, and was in use until 1860. By 1902 it had been converted into a shop, stores and blacksmith's forge. Although the location is unknown by the author, it is likely to have been sited on the sharp bend opposite the church where a smithy is marked on the 1888 Ordnance Survey. There was also a malthouse at Trelleck recorded in 1847 and a maltster at Tintern in 1842.

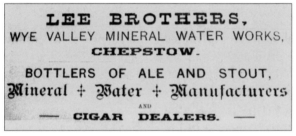

LEE BROTHERS,
WYE VALLEY MINERAL WATER WORKS,
CHEPSTOW.

BOTTLERS OF ALE AND STOUT,
Mineral ✝ Water ✝ Manufacturers
AND
— CIGAR DEALERS. —

The Lee Brothers were bottling ale and stout in Chepstow in 1895

In Chepstow town, Thomas Jenkins and Henry Phillips were brewing and malting on a more commercial basis in 1830, and Jenkins, who was also a 'Merchant and Ship Owner,' continued the business in Bridge Street. However, in 1843 he leased 'All that brewery situated in Bridge Street in the town of Chepstow with dwelling house and yard lately converted to a country house and warehouse with implements' to James Dowle. From 1859 Phillip Creese was a brewer in Nelson Street, joined by Thomas Creese in 1862 an 'ale and porter merchant and soda water and lemonade manufacturer' in St Mary's Street. By 1871 Creese was still brewing with George Mereweather at the Gate House, but they were competing with Arnold & Co.'s agent in Welsh Street from the Wickwar Brewery.

Arnold & Co. was founded in 1820 at Wickwar in Avon, and during the 1880s took over the Gloucestershire brewery of H. & A. Perrett, thus becoming Arnold Perrett & Co. Ltd. with an agent and stores in Albion Square, Chepstow. The stores were acquired by the Stroud Brewery in 1924 who advertised 'Beers worth drinking, Wines and Spirits of maturity and Aerated Waters of quality'. However, in 1962 the premises were taken over by West Country Breweries.

Wine was a very different trade with a dependency on imports rather than produced goods. In Roman times wine was imported in amphoræ, but by the Saxon period imported and home produced wines were available, with monasteries and priories tending their own vineyards. When Heath referred to the estate called the Vineyard at Monmouth he wrote:

> Now it is a question with me. Whether or not the Vine was ever cultivated here in the open, at any period of time, - much more so early as in the reign of Henry 111 ... So little wine was used in England, that in 1386 the best sort, sold at 20s. the ton, and the second best at 13s. 4d. – previous to which period [1300] it was only sold by Apothecaries as a Cordial.

According to Kissack in the 13th century 'Wine cost 1s. 6d. a hogshead and, although there was a vineyard at Osbaston, most wine seems to have come through Tintern where it cost twopence a day for storage'. At Chepstow there was apparently a vineyard in the priory grounds. In 2006 the Monnow Valley Vineyard at Osbaston and the Parva Farm Vineyard at Tintern were both producing Welsh wines.

From the 12th century wine was imported from France to Chepstow which enjoyed a long association with the wine trade, and from the 15th century French, German and Portuguese wines were shipped in casks from Bristol and along the Severn to Newnham and on the Wye to Chepstow. The Chepstow Society's *Trail* informs those interested that: 'From medieval times to the late 19th century Chepstow had a flourishing wine trade with ships sailing from here to Bordeaux, Spain and Portugal' and during the 18th century this trade was supported by cork cutters and glass blowers recorded in Chepstow parish registers.

The Worshipful Company of Vintners was established in 1364, but this was a name almost unheard of outside London where they were based. However, in both Chepstow and Ross vintners were recorded on monuments in the 17th century. The meaning of the word has almost been lost and replaced by wine merchant to signify a person selling wine. In the time of Queen Anne the following song was sung:

> Come, come, let us drink the Vintner's health;
> 'Tis the cask, not the coffer, that holds the true wealth;
> If to founders of blessing we pyramids raise;
> The bowl, not the sceptre, deserves the best praise.
> Then next to the Queen, let the Vintner's fame shine;
> She gives us good laws, and they fill us good wine.

By the mid-17th century there was a growing taste for spirits which led to the popularity of gin and excessive drinking in the 18th century, when according to Hackwood:

Everybody drank, and nobody drank moderately; the vice was common to all, rich and poor alike. At social parties no gentleman ever thought of leaving the table sober; the host would have considered it a slight on his hospitality. Even ladies and clergymen sometimes got drunk, and intoxication was so common a thing it passed without remark. The upper classes drank wine, and every man among them liked to boast himself a 'two-bottle man'; and even if he could not consume that quantity, he could at least drink till he fell beneath the table.

WINES AND SPIRITS FOR EVERY-DAY USE
Selected from W & A Gilbey's List of 200 varieties.

The seals and labels on all WINES and SPIRITS bottled by W & A GILBEY may be accepted as an absolute guarantee of their purity and genuineness. Under the Act of Parliament 38 & 39 Vic., Cap. 63, the purity of any Wine or Spirit can be verified on application to the Local Government Analyst.

This "SELECTED LIST" of W & A GILBEY'S WINES AND SPIRITS comprises two descriptions only of each class of Wines and Spirits, the first selected on account of its moderate price, and the second for its fine quality combined with greater age.

Agent—

G. FREEMAN, *Grocer*
CHURCH STREET, MONMOUTH

WINES

			Per Bott.	Per Doz.
PORT Castle 1A	.. ..	4 years old	1/9	21/
PORT Castle B	.. ..	8 years old	2/4	28/
SPANISH PORT Castle 1	..	2 years old	1/3	15/
SPANISH PORT Castle 4	..	10 years old	1/10	22/
SHERRY Castle SPANISH	..	2 years old	1/3	15/
SHERRY Castle C *Pale*	..	6 years old	2/4	28/
MARSALA Castle VP *Pale*	..	3 years old	1/4	16/
MARSALA Castle C *Pale*	..	7 years old	1/8	20/
CLARET Castle A	*Upwards of a year in bottle*		1/	12/
CLARET Castle C	*Upwards of a year in bottle*		1/6	18/
SAUMUR Castle *Silver Foil*	.. ..	..	2/1	25/
SAUMUR Castle *Gold Foil* ..	.. ..	..	2/6	30/
CHAMPAGNE Castle 1	.. ..	..	2/2	26/
CHAMPAGNE Castle 3	.. ..	..	3/6	42/

SPIRITS

			Per Bott.	Per Doz.
GIN Castle UP	33 *under proof*		2/	24/
GIN Castle Proof	*proof*		2/10	34/
IRISH WHISKEY Castle UP	33 *under proof*		2/3	27/
IRISH WHISKEY Castle DO	*proof*		3/3	39/
SCOTCH WHISKEY Castle UP	33 *under proof*		2/3	27/
SCOTCH WHISKEY Castle SO	*proof*		3/3	39/
BRANDY Castle UP	33 *under proof*		2/3	27/
BRANDY Castle Proof	*proof*		3/	36/
COGNAC Castle D	33 *under proof*		3/	36/
COGNAC Castle FO	*proof*		4/9	57/
JAMAICA RUM Castle UP	33 *under proof*		2/3	27/
JAMAICA RUM Castle JO	*proof*		3/3	39/
HOLLANDS Castle 1	14 *under proof*		2/4	28/
HOLLANDS *(Silver Stream)*	14 *under proof*		2/8	32/

All Bottles (except for Sparkling Wines) are charged 1d. each, which is allowed when returned.

Gilbey's 1879 price list

The lower classes drank beer when they did not drink gin, and it was a common thing among working men to drink three or four quarts of strong, heavy ale each day of their lives. In 1761 an attempt to raise the price of ale to $3^{1}/_{2}$d. a quart was successfully resisted by the public.

From the late 18th century T. Taylor of Carmarthen was importing 'Old Red and White Port Wines of the best quality' into the Port of Bristol, Purchas from Fownhope was advertising 'French Brandy, Jamaica and other Spirituous Liquors', and Gardner in Gloucester was selling a range of wine, port, madeira, claret, champagne from France, Portugal, South Africa and the West Indies, so it is not surprising to discover that in 1769 John Powell of Monmouth founded his wine and spirit business in Agincourt Square about fifty years before James Hall at Redbrook. The Powell's wine and spirit

BRITISH WINE.

Notice to all persons holding Excise licences authorising the sale for consumption on or off the premises of Foreign Wine or British Wine, or the manufacture of British Wine.

---

1. The Commissioners of His Majesty's Customs and Excise in pursuance of the Regulations, a copy of which is appended, made by them on the 31st January, 1928, under Section 10 of the Finance Act, 1911, which prescribe, among other matters, that British Wine, to which Foreign Wine has been added by the manufacturer in the course of manufacture, must not be sold or exposed for sale otherwise than under the designation of a British Wine, hereby give notice that :—

(a) Such wine must in all cases be described as a British Wine. If it is desired to indicate that Foreign Wine has been added in the course of manufacture it must be stated that the proportion does not exceed that allowed by the Statutory Regulations, viz., 15 gallons in every 115 gallons of the product.

(b) All bottles in which such wine is sold or exposed for sale must in future bear a distinct and conspicuous indication that the wine has been manufactured in the United Kingdom.

2. The Commissioners also call the special attention of all persons concerned to No. 2 of the Regulations in question, under which a dealer in or retailer of Foreign Wine or British Wine must not mix for sale any Foreign Wine with any British Wine ; and to No. 6 of the Regulations, which states that Foreign Wine includes all wine imported into the United Kingdom.

3. Any person contravening the Regulations is liable to a penalty of £50.

Notice No. 44.

BY ORDER OF THE COMMISSIONERS OF CUSTOMS
AND EXCISE.

Custom House, London E.C.3.

February, 1928.

Changes in the regulations. It would appear that up to 15 gallons of foreign wine could be added to 115 gallons of British Wine without necessarily telling the customer. But it still had to be called British Wine

JOHN MASTERS,

WINE & SPIRIT MERCHANT

AND DEALER IN

LONDON AND DUBLIN STOUT,

BURTON ALES, ETC.,

MONNOW STREET, MONMOUTH.

John Masters was trading in Monmouth in 1862

business descended through the family with C. Powell in 1888 selling Champagnes including 'Ayala's First Quality' and 'Heidsiecks's Dry Monopole' – the latter at 84s. per dozen bottles. It can still be purchased today but the price is now approximately £170 per case. The Powells were still trading into the 20th century.

In the 1890s there was a family grocer and wine and spirit importer in Agincourt Square run by William Hall who claimed being 'established upwards of a century'. He could have been a descendant of the James Hall from Redbrook who continued as a wine and spirit merchant in Monmouth after he ceased brewing. In 1948 William Hall & Co. were supplying a variety of food and drink including wines and mineral water. At this date mineral water, to cater for the more temperate drinker, was manufactured by C. N. Ballinger, who since the 1890s was known for 'Ballinger's Famous Mineral Waters' from the Pont Mynwy Mineral Water Works.

At Chepstow during the 18th century there were two noted wine merchants – Thomas Powis, who died in 1716 after trading as a vintner in London, and Richard Fydell, 'well known for the excellent red port he imported direct from Oporto, Portugal' in the 1780s. It was around this period that Grahame Farr in his book *Chepstow Ships* noted:

> it is strange that there are few references in the registers illustrating the wine trade, apart from records of shareholding by the Fydells, James Dowle, Thomas Mutlow, Joseph Davis and John Jones, all described as wine or spirit merchants.

It was probably around this period that the vaulted cellars of Raglan House were used for wine storage.

Records exist of John Bowsher, James Hodges and Richard Watkins in 1813 as 'Wine Merchants and Carpenters' at Quince Garden, of James Davis, a spirit dealer in 1830, and Joseph Davies, a wine merchant in the High Street from the 1830s to the 1900s. There was also the Chepstow Wine & Spirit Co. Ltd. at the Back during the 1840s. Part of the old priory cellars were used as a bonded warehouse, where Dowle and Sandford, wine and spirit merchants, later trading as Sandford & Co. were based until 1870. They were followed by Miller Bros. with Dobell, Mott & Co. listed there in 1901. Two other Wine Merchants worth mentioning in Chepstow were Edwin Ellis, agent for W.A. Gilbey and Price who were selling 'Half Guinea Hampers' containing '1 bottle Old Cognac Brandy, 1 bottle Fine Irish or Scotch Whisky, 1 bottle Old Port, 1 bottle Fine Sherry' for the Christmas market in 1897.

> To exalt, enthrone, establish and defend,
> To welcome home mankind's mysterious friend:
> Wine, true begetter of all arts that be;
> Wine, privilege of the completely free;
> Wine the recorder; Wine the sagely strong;
> Wine, bright avenger of sly-dealing wrong –
> Awake, Ausonian Muse, and sing the vineyard song!
>
> (H.Belloc)

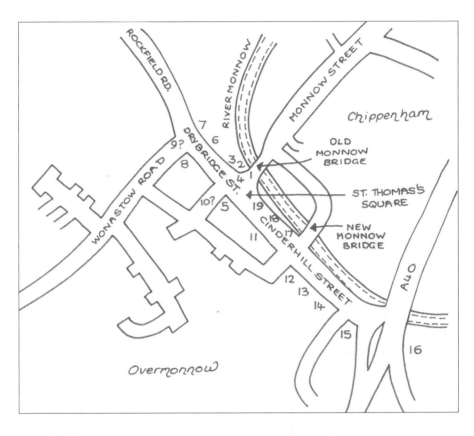

1. Bell	14. Cherry Tree
2. Plough	15. Railway Tavern
3. Full Moon	16. Refreshment Room
4. Troy House	17. Fox
5. **Green Dragon**	18. Oak
6. **Three Horse Shoes**	19. Bee Hive
7. **Britannia**	
8. Red Lion/Lion	Uncertain positions:
9. Globe	Victoria
10. Bagot House	Three Compasses
11. **Rising Sun/ Riverside Inn**	
12. Albion	
13. White Horse	**Bold** open in 2007

MONMOUTH – Chapter 3: Monnow Bridge and Overmonnow

CHAPTER THREE

Monmouth:
MONNOW BRIDGE & OVERMONNOW

The market town of Monmouth lies on the eastern boundary of Wales in the old county of Monmouthshire. Although present day Monmouth has grown and expanded, the heart of the town still enjoys a pleasing location between the rivers Wye and Monnow, and below the hills of the Forest of Dean, the rolling countryside of Herefordshire and the wooded hills of Monmouthshire and the Wye Valley. Earlier administration has led to the notion that Monmouth was not Welsh, but local government organisation of 1972 firmly established the town in Welsh Gwent, and further changes have placed Monmouth in the county of that name.

Monmouth's fascinating history dates from Roman times when a settlement known as *Blestium* was established, but it was not until the Norman period that its history really began. The Normans took advantage of a well-defended site between the two rivers, where they built their castle, established a market and founded a priory. Visible evidence of these may be seen today, but the most prominent survivor from the past is the Monnow Bridge reflecting the town's medieval status. With Monmouth's situation not just on the great road from London to South Wales, but also having access to a navigable river, it is not surprising that the town flourished and developed.

According to Archdeacon Coxe's *Historical Tour in Monmouthshire* published in 1801:

> There are no Manufactures, excepting the iron works of Partridge and Company; the inhabitants are principally supported by the navigation of the Wy, the trade with Hereford and Bristol, the supply of the neighbouring districts with various kinds of shop goods, and the influx of company. Among the articles brought down the river, which give employment to many of the inhabitants, bark must not be omitted; it is conveyed in large quantities from the forests of the Upper Wy, and landed on the banks, where after being pared and cleansed, it is sent for exportation to Chepstow.

Later historians have added the industries of brickmaking, ship-building, agriculture, corn milling and trades associated with timber and coal.

During the 18th century the turnpike trusts began to improve the public roads which Charles Heath, Monmouth's own antiquarian, bookseller and printer, described as:

> often impassable, owing to the floods; and travellers compelled to remain here three or four days, till the waters had retired within their proper bounds [others being] in a dreadful state, being full of large rocks and loose stones, that render it dangerous both to horse and foot passengers ... Such indeed was the narrowness of the roads, that to every waggon a boy was attached, as an avant courier, who preceded the team a considerable way, blowing all the time a large horn, to give notice to those travelling the same line to halt where they could pass with mutual convenience.

Due to the bad state of the roads, transportation on the Wye was often a preferred choice, especially for heavy goods. Since time immemorial the Wye had been navigable, but it was not until the 17th century that a serious effort was made to establish it as a commercial waterway. It was a difficult river to navigate, but its untamed beauty attracted writers, artists, and poets seeking the Picturesque in the 18th and early 19th centuries. The trip down the river became known as the *Wye Tour*, which became commercialised by the boat proprietors and innkeepers and led to the start of tourism in Monmouth. Since then this has been a major industry and by 1946 guide books attracted visitors to:

> The ancient county borough of Monmouth ... though an important market town and the shopping centre for a population many miles beyond its boundaries, has a quaint medieval air. Change seems to have no place here, and a very restful air is the dominant note of the place.

After 1755, road improvements were gradually carried out by the Monmouth Turnpike Trust, and although a fairly reliable form of transport remained downstream on the Wye its use began to decline after the opening of the railway offering cheaper and quicker communications to Usk from 1857, to Ross from 1873, and down the Wye Valley to Chepstow from 1876. In more recent times the railways have closed and road transport has rapidly taken over, with many unacceptable developments such as the building of the A40 dual-carriageway road, which completely separates the town of Monmouth from the river Wye.

Notable persons associated with Monmouth include: the 12th-century historian Geoffrey of Monmouth; King Henry V, who was born at the castle in 1387; Lord Nelson, who visited the town in 1802; and Charles

Rolls, the aviator and co-founder of Rolls Royce. Monmouth has not forgotten these men – outside the Shire Hall there are statues to Henry V and Charles Rolls, an oriel window at the Priory is called Geoffrey's Window, and Nelson is commemorated in the name of the museum. Also several talented historians have written at length about Monmouth, including Archdeacon Coxe, Sir J.A. Bradney, Charles Heath and, more recently, Keith Kissack. Their carefully researched books and pamphlets now line the shelves in the local library and museum.

Despite being in Wales, Monmouth remains anglicised with its historic schools, Shire Hall, churches and chapels, and fine Georgian buildings. Today the bustling market town has a welcoming and relaxing atmosphere where a good selection of inns, hotels, guest-houses and tea rooms offer refreshment and hospitality to visitor and resident alike. A variety of shops are clustered around Church Street and Agincourt Square, and line the wide Monnow Street leading down to the unique Monnow Bridge.

Monnow Bridge was constructed for defence with a gate tower standing on the bridge itself. The present structure was built of stone in the 1270s to replace an earlier wooden bridge. At the turn of the 13th century it formed part of the new town defences, and throughout the centuries has served as a porter's lodge, a dwelling house, a guard room, a lock-up, and a storeroom. It was originally a toll bridge with payments in 1296 ranging from 1 *obol* for every horse, mare and cow for sale; skins per 100 – 1d.; a cart of salt – 1d.; a cask of wine and ashes 3 *obols*; a vat and leaden

cooling trough for brew[ing] – 1 *obol*; 100 salmon, mullets, congers and a dozen eels, salted – 1d. The *obol* was worth ¹/₂d., whilst the wine and ashes were probably used by the church for certain festivals.

In 1705 the bridge was conveyed to the sons of James Bibee, an innholder, and was described in the deed as 'All That peece of building comonly called Monnow gate Situated on Monnow Bridge within the said Towns and the Office of Porter of the said Gate'. A lean-to extension was added which projected over the bridge and, although not documented, it may have served as the **Bell Inn**, portrayed in an early

The Bell Inn next to the Monnow Bridge c.1805

St. Thomas's Square, Overmonnow and the Monnow Bridge c.1900
(painting by John Arthur Evans)

19th-century painting by John Crome. According to deeds of 1725, John Humphreys, an innholder, and John Bird, a blacksmith, were occupying a 'Messuage with one shop, 1 curtillage, 1 workhouse, 1 backside, with 2 gardens adjoining the bridge called Monnow Bridge'. By 1805 this unnamed public house and brewhouse had closed, and like the elusive **Bell** left no trace of its existence.

Due to an increase in horse-drawn traffic it became necessary to widen the bridge and provide a pedestrian passage, so the lean-to was removed around 1819, and another passageway was inserted during the 1840s. In order to protect the Monnow Bridge from the ever increasing traffic, plans to replace the bridge began in the 1920s, but it was not until 2004 that a new bridge was constructed a few hundred yards downstream. The ancient Monnow Bridge has since been closed to traffic so that those on foot can walk over the river Monnow and admire the bridge at leisure.

On the south-eastern side of the Monnow Bridge is a populated area known as Overmonnow. According to Charles Heath in 1804:

> The inhabitants at large are induced to believe, that the Over Monnow town had existed long before that which we now consider as the principal part of Monmouth, – because the bridge, the gateway, the church, the moat, etc. are such evident monuments of its high antiquity.

This was confirmed by another historian, Sir Joseph Bradney, a hundred years later:

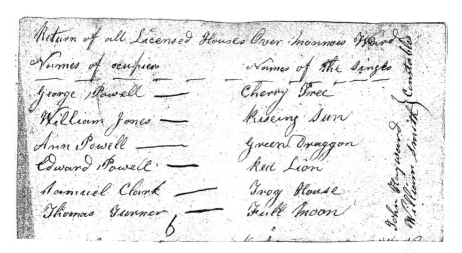

The Return of all six licensed houses in Over Monnow in 1835

The suburb of Over Monnow is considered to be the site of the most ancient part of the town, and it is perhaps on this side of the Monnow that the Roman town of *Blestium* stood. The ancient earth-work called *Clawdd Du* (the black dyke) which encircles the town is probably the boundary fence of the first town that was built here.

The church referred to is dedicated to St. Thomas and dates from the 12th century, whilst recent excavations have revealed Roman artefacts at Overmonnow.

Heath also added that Over Monnow was known as the 'Cappers Town', where a certain style of woollen caps had been manufactured since the days of Henry V which were known as Monmouth Caps. Recent research has not found any records of this trade at Over Monnow, but the tradition must stem from some grain of truth. In 1801 Archdeacon Coxe wrote:

Caps were once a considerable branch of trade in Monmouth. In the days of Henry the Fifth, and in subsequent times, Monmouth caps were much esteemed. Fluellen, in Shakespeare's *Henry the Fifth*, alluding to this fashion, addresses the King and said "If your majesties is remember'd of it, the Welshmen did goot service in a garden where leeks did grow, wearing leeks in their Monmouth caps".

At the beginning of the 18th century 11 licensed premises were recorded in Over Monnow; after a dip in numbers this grew to 13 open in the mid-19th century, but slowly declined to the present four that offer food and drink in the 21st century. Most of the past pubs and beer houses were situated in Cinderhill Street with a few in Drybridge Street and St. Thomas's Square.

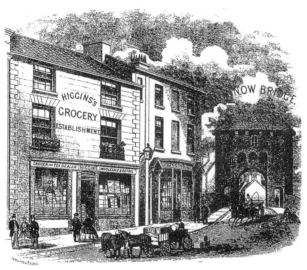

The one-time Plough became Higgins Grocery towards the end of the 19th century

The former Full Moon

Two former pubs once stood on the west side of the Monnow Bridge in St. Thomas's Square. Next to the bridge was the **Plough**, which was open in the 1850s when William Cook was the landlord. He was followed by William Watts and in 1871 John Griffiths probably served as the last landlord. After this the multi-trading George Higgins took over the premises and the adjoining building as a 'grocer, provision & flour dealer' as well as agent for W. & A. Gilbey, wine and spirit merchants, which continued into the 20th century.

On the same side of St. Thomas Square, only a door away, was the **Full Moon**, which was an earlier establishment dating from at least 1792 when John Watkins was recorded as the innkeeper. In 1804 the licence was transferred from Charles Hughes to Richard Watkins and Joseph Morris, and around 1826 a Female Friendly Society met at the inn. From thereon a succession of publicans kept the **Full Moon** until it was acquired by the Burghams of Redbrook Brewery who closed it in the early 1900s.

On the corner of St. Thomas's Square and Drybridge Street, but now lost to redevelopment, was **Troy House**. It was known as a meeting place of Radicals in the 1820s and '30s when Thomas Worgan was the innkeeper

St. Thomas's Square about 1910 with Troy House right of centre

issuing beer tokens. Apart from the Clarkes serving beer for three decades after Mr. Worgan, there was a succession of innkeepers until Edgar Thomas took over in the early 20th century. He appears to have been the last landlord before the house closed.

Almost opposite on the corner of Goldwire Lane is the **Green Dragon**, the longest surviving pub in Overmonnow and established on a site of archaeological interest. In 1998 an archaeological evaluation was carried out on land behind the inn, which revealed finds dating from medieval times including sherds of cooking utensils, and also clay pipe stems from the 18th and 19th centuries. The report concluded that the 'site was extensively disturbed by excavations to recover iron slag during the 17th and 18th centuries. These excavations removed all earlier archaeological features except for two shallow hollows in the surface of the natural'.

The Green Dragon in the flood of 1889

The Green Dragon in 2005

The **Green Dragon** in St. Thomas's Square was established as an inn at some time before 1801 when the keys for St. Thomas's church were kept there. In the 1830s beer tokens were issued by Thomas Powell, the licensee, who was followed by other members of his family including Ann and Margaret. Later, James Gwilliam kept the pub for a couple of decades, after which there was a succession of different landlords. At the beginning of the 21st century the **Green Dragon**, despite its name, was painted white and now offers live entertainment on certain nights of the week. A Red Lion is a symbol of Wales, whereas the Green Dragon sign is usually associated with the English St. George and the Dragon. However, it is also represented in the arms of the Earl of Pembroke.

From St. Thomas's Square a walk along the north side of Drybrook Street leads to the **Three Horse Shoes**, which was originally run by a blacksmith, William Phillips, in the second half of the 19th century. William Phillips had opened his forge by 1859 in Drybrook Street, but it was not until the 1880s that he opened the adjoining property aptly called the **Three Horse Shoes Inn**. In 1923 Osbert Wheeler was the publican, and Victor Mackie, a horse breaker, was occupying the Three Horse Shoes Yard. In recent times the inn has been refurbished and, with its satellite television, caters for football enthusiasts. Although the **Three Horse Shoes** seems an

The Three Horse Shoes in Drybrook Street in 2005

odd number for shoes that come in sets of four, it has been suggested that a sign depicting three horse shoes indicates to unfortunate travellers on horse-back, that a blacksmith was available to replace a cast shoe.

On the same side of Drybrook Street stands the **Britannia**, known to have existed in 1835 under the supervision of John Pembridge, who was followed by Maria Pembridge. Since then the pub has managed to remain open under a long list of licensees. The Britannia is a common pub name throughout the country, but there are various explanations. The obvious one is the figure of Britannia that, until recently, graced some British coinage. The original model for the figure, which was used on a medal struck in 1665, was Frances Stewart, a mistress of Charles II and later Duchess of Richmond. The Royal Navy has made use of the name since 1682, and many pub signs, especially along the coast, include a ship on their sign. The one oddity is a pub in London which refers to the survey of the British Isles originally published in 1588 by the antiquarian, William Camden, and called *Britannia*.

The Britannia in 2005

A short-lived pub once existed in the mid-19th century at Overmonnow known as the **Victoria**. Its whereabouts is unknown, but it may have been housed in Victoria Cottage which is near the **Britannia**, or in a house opposite the Infant School, giving its name to the adjoining Victoria Estate in Wonastow Road.

On the corner of Drybrook Street and Wonastow Road is the Old Toll House, a reminder of when this road to Abergavenny was turnpiked by the Monmouth Trust who realigned the route to avoid wading through water at all seasons of the year. Near the former toll house stands an imposing building with steps which housed the **Red Lion**, an inn kept by Edward Powell in 1830. He remained there for around twenty years, but trade eventually declined and the **Red Lion** (known

The one-time Red Lion in 2005

40

locally simply as the **Lion** in 1910) closed in the 1920s – James Meadows being recorded as the innkeeper in 1923.

At an unknown site in Drybrook Street was the **Globe** of 1744, which by 1833 had become a private dwelling occupied by James Middleton. It was reopened as the **Old Globe** by Susan Gwilliam in 1862, and referred to as 'the old Globe in Drybrook Street' after it had closed in 1877. The Globe is a fairly common inn sign originating in Portugal on taverns selling the country's wines. The name was also used by landlords to suggest 'a man of the world' who had decided to end his days as an innkeeper.

Leading in a westerly direction from St. Thomas's Square is Goldwire Lane, known as Goldsmith's Lane in the early 18th century. Somewhere near Bagot Cottage was a cider house called **Bagot House**. This probably replaced the former **Lion** of the 1830s when the eastern stretch of Goldwire Lane was called Lion Lane.

From St. Thomas's Square a dramatically changed Cinderhill Street leads above the River Monnow to join the fast and noisy A40 dual-carriageway. A glance at the 1917 Ordnance Survey map reveals a long line of buildings along the riverside which have since been demolished to provide a riverside car park. Cinderhill was named after the piles of cinders deposited there from the medieval forges, which from the 17th century proved to be a valuable asset to the Forest of Dean iron works, as described by Andrew Yarranton in his *Improvement by Sea and Land* written in 1698:

> And in the Forest of Deane and thereabouts, and as high as Worcester, there are great and infinite quantities of these Cinders, some in vast Mounts above ground, some under ground, which will supply the Iron-works some hundreds of years, and these Cinders are they which make the prime best Iron, and with much less Charcoal than doth the Iron Stone.

In the past Cinderhill Street housed a number of pubs and beer houses; – some were demolished on the river side of the street and others sites have been redeveloped during the 20th century. The only remaining licensed premises is the **Riverside Hotel**, originally known as the **Rising Sun** from at least 1822 up to the 1980s. There was also a **Sun** recorded in 1717 which may have become the **Rising Sun** at a later date. In 1831 beer tokens were issued by the licensee, William Jones, as part of his efforts during the parliamentary elections. Various landlords by the names of Howells, Watkins, Symonds, Mills, Lewis and Underwood kept the **Rising Sun** from the 1840s to more recent times; then in 1972 the **Rising Sun Motel** was opened. It was run by John and Florence Poyner who offered

The Rising Sun Inn became a Motel in 1972

The bar at the Riverside Hotel
(photo courtesy of Riverside Hotel)

to 'do their utmost to make your stay happy and comfortable' in their well appointed motel with 'a pleasant restaurant in the lovely old town of Monmouth. An excellent centre for touring, fishing and pony trekking in the beautiful Wye Valley'. Shortly after this the motel was renamed the **Riverside Hotel** offering 'friendly service and a warm welcome, good food and wines, comfortable rooms and great value for money'.

On the same side of Cinderhill Street is a modern shop with an off licence which replaced the former

The Riverside Hotel in 2005

Albion beer house that was run by the Morgan family from the mid-19th century. In 1904 Fanny Morgan was selling beer there that was obtained from the Burgham's brewery at Redbrook. A little later the **Albion** closed and became the Model Lodging House kept by James Read in 1937.

Just south of the **Albion** were two other pubs which flourished in the 19th century – the **White Horse** and the **Cherry Tree**. There was a **White Horse** recorded from 1719 to 1792 which may have been the same licensed premises as the inn of the same name in the 1850s, when its bad reputation was described in the *Merlin* newspaper as 'the house of pollution, drunkenness and all but murder'. The article continued:

> a number of that hitherto well-conducted regiment, the Monmouth Militia, led astray by bad characters of the other sex, after an evening spent in drunkenness and debauchery, returned at four in the morning to the White Horse (which is famed for its notorious character) demanding admission. On meeting refusal, bayonets were drawn, one man was stabbed in the arm, and a regular riot ensued until eight drill sergeants appeared with drawn swords to quell the disturbance.

The **White Horse** pub name has been in use since the 15th century as an heraldic sign, representing the horse in the arms of the guilds of coachmen, farriers, innholders, saddlers and wheelwrights. Of course, it is commonly known in equestrian circles that a white horse, unless an albino, is always called a grey.

The *Merlin* also reported on the following case held at the Petty Sessions in March 1855:

> John Howell, who keeps a cider house on the Cinder-hill, was charged with having drawn cider, for sale, before half-past 12-o'clock on Sunday week. There was some doubt as to whether it was not half-past twelve o'clock when the defendant was seen to have drawn the cider, the evidence on both sides being very conflicting as to time – the defendant was therefore ordered to pay the expenses.

This description would doubtless have referred to the cider house and shop kept by John Howell in 1862.

At the southern end of Cinderhill Street was the **Cherry Tree**, dating from the 18th century and named after the nearby cherry orchards. In the 1830s the inn was kept by George Powell, another landlord who issued beer tokens during the parliamentary elections of 1831. George was followed by Thomas Herbert who was there in 1863 when the Ancient Order of Foresters Friendly Society met at the hostelry. In 1899 the licensed house was sold by the Duke of Beaufort and purchased by Francis Wintle of the Forest Brewery at Mitcheldean. The brewery made an inventory and valuation of the **Cherry**

Tree in 1901 when the tenancy changed from W. Olliver to J.W. Hooper. The pub then consisted of a tap room, bar and skittle alley with bedrooms above and cellars below. There was a large quantity of stock including bottles of whisky, brandy, claret, lime juice and casks of beer – the total amount of the stock, effects and licence coming to £269 5s. 4d. It was probably during William Watkins' tenancy in the 1920s that the **Cherry Tree** was described by the brewery as 'poor'. In 1937 it was taken over by the Cheltenham Original Brewery as:

> ALL THAT Inn messuages stables and premises known as the Cherry Tree situate and being Number 63 Cinderhill Street Monmouth. TOGETHER with two cottages adjoining the same premises and also the orchard and garden at rear containing two roods thirteen perches or there-abouts now in the occupation of John Church.

Apparently the **Cherry Tree** remained open until 1963, after which it was demolished.

At the bottom of Cinderhill Street, the existing garage is built on the site of the former **Railway Tavern**, which was trading at least a year before the opening of the Pontypool and Usk to Monmouth Railway in 1857. Henry Williams was the forward-thinking landlord who captured the train passengers going to and from Troy Station for many years before the station's own **Refreshment Room** was granted a six-day licence in 1887. This obviously took some trade away from the **Railway**, which appears to have closed shortly after Florence Davies served as landlady in 1907. The **Refreshment Room** at Troy Station remained open until the line closed in 1964, despite an alarming but amusing incident that occurred in 1916. This was retold by E.T. Davies and Keith Kissack in their *Inns and Friendly Societies of Monmouth* published in 1981:

> the horse drawing the King's Head omnibus started on its return journey with four passengers inside quite unaware that the driver was still in the Refreshment Room. They found out when the horse, after passing the water-trough in St. Thomas's Square, collided with the band of Royal Monmouthshire Royal Engineers, leading a draft for France as they emerged from Monnow Bridge.

After the closure of the railway, the station site was re-used as a road haulage depot and coal yard and Troy station building was eventually dismantled and then carefully reassembled in 1990 at Winchcombe on the Gloucestershire and Warwickshire Railway to replace a similar one that had been demolished.

The river side of Cinderford Street housed three licensed premises in the mid-19th century. In 1832 Thomas Wilks applied for a licence for a

Above: Troy Station about 1900

Left: Mrs. N. Wallett, who served in the Refreshment Room at Troy Station until it closed in 1959

'Beer House known by the sign of the Fox and which is intended to be kept as an Inn, Alehouse or Victuallers House'. It was well established by 1856 when George Harris was the publican. He was followed by Charles Lee, who must have been unsuccessful, for the licence for the **Fox** was not renewed in 1882. The **Fox** is an uncommon name for an inn in the Welsh borders, but has been in use for several centuries. The name is often coupled with other animals and may have derived from the verse that includes:

> I am a crafty fox, you see
> But there is no harm in me
> My master he has placed me here
> To let you know he sells good beer

The **Oak** and the **Bee Hive**, which faced the **Rising Sun** (now the **Riverside**), were known to have thrived in the 1850s. Henry Castree established the **Oak** by combining two houses into one around 1855, but no further records have been found. The same lack of information applies to the **Bee Hive**.

45

In 1771 there is mention of a carpenter digging for cinders in the garden of the **Three Compasses**. The site of this pub is unknown, but as it was associated with cinders it could well have been situated in Cinderhill, although other 'cinder' sites existed in and around Monmouth. It is perhaps coincidental that the sign of the **Three Compasses** represents the arms of the guilds of carpenters together with joiners and masons. Three pairs of compasses specifically referring to the carpenters.

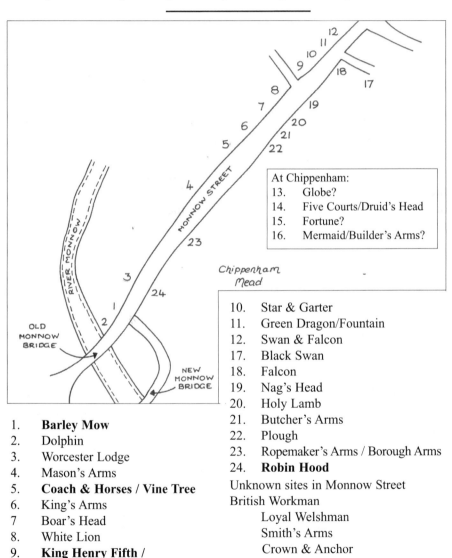

At Chippenham:
13. Globe?
14. Five Courts/Druid's Head
15. Fortune?
16. Mermaid/Builder's Arms?

10. Star & Garter
11. Green Dragon/Fountain
12. Swan & Falcon
17. Black Swan
18. Falcon
19. Nag's Head
20. Holy Lamb
21. Butcher's Arms
22. Plough
23. Ropemaker's Arms / Borough Arms
24. **Robin Hood**

1. **Barley Mow**
2. Dolphin
3. Worcester Lodge
4. Mason's Arms
5. **Coach & Horses / Vine Tree**
6. King's Arms
7 Boar's Head
8. White Lion
9. **King Henry Fifth /
    Gloucestershire House**

Unknown sites in Monnow Street
British Workman
  Loyal Welshman
  Smith's Arms
  Crown & Anchor
Bold open in 2007

MONMOUTH – Chapter 4: Monnow Street and Chippenham

CHAPTER FOUR

Monmouth:
MONNOW STREET & CHIPPENHAM

In 1907, before cars, vans and lorries filled the streets of Monmouth, Joseph Bradney, the antiquarian, wrote 'The approach from the Monnow Gate up Monnow Street is striking, on account of the width of the street'. It was a typical market street with suffrecent width for animals and stalls in the middle and gated at each narrow end. Monnow Street is of ancient origin with its name dating from at least the mid-13th century, and is where archaeologists have unearthed Roman, Saxon, Norman and Medieval artefacts. According to Charles Heath it was:

> originally a barbarous holloway, as deep as a horse's back, – and on each side of the footpath were a number of Wells, that supplied the inhabitants with water ... It was scarcely passable for a horse carrying a pair of pots, from the narrowness of the way to enter the Market place, – and waggons seldom attempted it, except when loaded with timber, on account of the difficulty of turning into the Back-lane.

The Back Lane is now known as St. John's Street.

In recent years the character of the southern end of Monnow Street has dramatically changed, with traffic now rerouted over the new Monnow bridge, the closure of the cattle market and the construction of large car parks for town and supermarket shoppers, the latter overshadowing Chippenham Mead. This open space was much admired by Archdeacon Coxe in 1801 when he wrote:

> The walks in the vicinity of Monmouth are extremely pleasant, particularly Chippenham meadow, which is a general rendezvous for company at the close of summer evenings; it is a flat oval plain, inclosed between the Wy, the Monnow, and the south side of the town; at the south-eastern extremity, the Monnow falls into the Wy, beneath a group of fine elms, which rise near the banks of the Trothy.

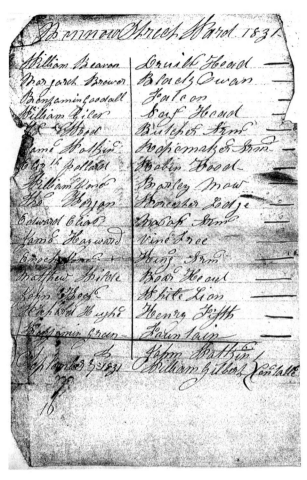

The Return of all licensed houses in
Monnow Street in 1835

Although still an attractive open space, criss-crossed by paths leading from Chippenhamgate Street to the banks of the Monnow, Chippenham Mead is now spoilt by the closeness of the A40 and its adjacent car parks. In the 18th century, popular horse-racing meetings that attracted all classes of society were held on Chippenham. A grandstand was erected for the two-day event and the inns in the town did a roaring trade. For various reasons the interest in the meetings gradually declined and they were held at Vauxhall, on the other side of the Monnow, between 1902 and 1914.

In 1722, Monnow Street boasted at least 22 licensed premises, 16 in 1832, 13 in 1835, but only four open in 2005. These four represent the thirty or so inns and inn names that have been recorded in the street over the centuries. Some flourished, others declined, a few changed names and several were demolished, so it is understandable that it has been a challenging task trying to locate them in Monnow and Chippenhamgate Streets.

On the west side of Monnow Street overlooking the old bridge is the **Gate House**, a relatively recent name for the former **Barley Mow**. This was established as a public house by 1812 when the Female Friendly Society met each month with its members each paying 3d. for refreshments and 1s. into the stock. This then paid out a small amount when the

1812 Rules for the Female Friendly Society at the Barley Mow

women were unable to work due to sickness, childbirth, accident or old age. From 1822, William Jones took over the license of the house 'known by the name or sign of the Barley Mow'. From thereon the Jones family dominated the running of the inn until the last quarter of the 19th century, after which the long list of licensees included the Teagues, Watkins, Steads and Harleys. When Mr. Teague was the landlord in 1887 the Loyal Trafalgar Lodge of Druids Friendly Society held their Jubilee Dinner at the **Barley Mow**, attended

The Barley Mow in its heyday

The Gate House was once the Barley Mow

by over 100 members. By 1939 Ind Coope & Allsopp were supplying Burton Ales to the pub which has continued to trade into the 21st century, although under a different name – the **Gate House**.

Between the **Barley Mow** and the old bridge stood a row of cottages until they were demolished in the 1950s. It is a possibility that these buildings could have been the site of the **Dolphin** of 1721, described in the will of Henry Barnes as a 'tenement with appurtenances in the town of Monmouth near Monnow Bridge called the Dolphin'. It may have been a later **Dolphin** that David Roberts kept for a brief period in the 1850s when it was reported that he hosted a dinner for the men of the constabulary in 1858.

Further up Monnow Street at number 107, recognised by its bay windows, was the former **Worcester Lodge**, run by Phillip Davies in

1830. This inn served its customers under a succession of publicans until Emily Morgan, who was licensee there during the 1920s and '30s, some time before it eventually closed around 1950.

Further up the street at number 69 was the **Mason's Arms**, which has a bundle of deeds dating from 1749 to 1872 at Gwent Record Office together with Francis Jones's will of 1875. He left the 'Messuage Dwelling House or Inn in which I now reside to my wife Eliza Jones'. James Jones was granted a licence for the **Mason's Arms** in 1822, and was a supporter of Joseph Price a Justice of the Peace and Deputy Lieutenant of the county. In 1824 an incident occurred at the inn which is described by E.T. Davies and Keith Kissack in their 1981 booklet *The Inns and Friendly Societies of Monmouth*:

Top: The Worcester Lodge about 1895
Below: New uses for the Worcester Lodge

Joseph Price assembled a rabble which, headed by the Militia band, attempted to break up the ball held at the Shire Hall by a mayor of whom he disproved. Having failed to disrupt the ball he led them round the town, the drunken band making disgusting noises outside the houses of his political opponents. At his subsequent trial it was alleged that whenever Mr. Price wished to promote any object by means of a mob, he invariably assembled them at the Mason's Arms, summoned the Militia NCOs, provided them all with drink, and led them forth in a body.

In 1839, during the Chartist arrests, the new landlord at the **Mason's Arms** was threatened with penalties by the mayor, unless he stopped

The one-time Mason's Arms (central)

serving beer to the men of the Chartist movement. Then in 1857 at the Mop Fair a large crowd at the **Mason's Arms** attacked a constable who, although joined by other members of his force, was unable to stop the fight; the report does not mention what part Thomas Powell, the publican, played in this affray. He was followed by a landlady by the name of Sibella Morgan and by the 20th century the inn was licensed to Lloyd and Yorath and tenanted to Elizabeth Morgan, who appears to have served as the last publican.

Almost midway up Monnow Street is the existing **Vine Tree**, originally called the **Coach and Horses**, one of the longest surviving inns in Monmouth. In 1792 Thomas Hill, a maltster, purchased a messuage for £360:

On the left is the Vine Tree with the King's Arms just before the second flag

where Timothy Morse formerly dwelt with malthouse, garden, yard and backside in Monnow Street ... which messuage has for many years past been divided and occupied as two tenements. One called the Coach and Horses now in occupation of Lewis Watkins and the other now in occupation of Abbe Davill as tenant.

Above: The Vine Tree in 2005. Below:The inn sign

Around 1820 the **Coach** or **Waggon and Horses** became known as the **Vine Tree** under the management of James Hayward. The 'Malthouse and Dry Malt Room' was occupied by John Tippins and the 'messuage adjoining' by John Farmer. In a will dated 1828 it appears that the two dwellings were combined to form a 'Public House called the Vine tree ... with the Brewhouse, Stables, Buildings, Cellars, Gardens etc. belonging'.

The conveyance of the **Vine Tree** and its associated buildings in 1842 provides a glimpse of the occupations of the tenants living at the rear of the inn – a gunsmith, a cabinet maker, a tailor, a flax dresser, a baker, a glazier and a tea dealer. The document also describes the 'advantage of a right of way leading from Monnow Street through the backside of the house of Joseph Shellard into and

TOWN OF MONMOUTH

TO BE
Sold by Auction,
BY MESSRS.

COURT AND SON

(Under a Power of Sale in a Mortgage Deed,) at the

BEAUFORT ARMS HOTEL, MONMOUTH,

On THURSDAY, the 16th day of APRIL, 1863,

At THREE o'clock in the Afternoon for FOUR precisely, subject to conditions of Sale:

ALL THAT

OLD-ESTABLISHED & WELL-ACCUSTOMED

PUBLIC HOUSE

CALLED THE

"BOAR'S HEAD INN,"

Situate in Monnow Street, in the Town of Monmouth, with the extensive Stabling Garden, and Orchard Ground lying behind the same, and now in the occupation of Mr. THOMAS HARVEY.

For further particulars, apply to Messrs. POWLES and EVANS, Solicitors, AUCTIONEERS, Monmouth.

Sale of the Boar's Head in 1863

out of the hereby granted messuages', plus a seat in the parish church. The **Vine Tree** changed ownership again in 1859 when Richard Jones, a maltster and brewer, purchased the inn for £720 and, with William Jones as innkeeper, kept the premises for many years. From the 1920s Albert Johnstone owned and occupied the inn until 1940 when the 'messuage or Inn known as the Vine Tree Inn and outbuildings erected thereon and Together with the right of way' was sold to the Alton Court Brewery at Ross. In 1962 it was taken over by West Country Breweries and eventually passed to Whitbread. In the 21st century the **Vine Tree** is a busy high street pub offering food, drink and football on TV in interesting old world surroundings.

Also on the west side of Monnow Street there was once the **King's Arms**, an important 18th-century inn with stabling. Thomas Williams, innkeeper, and David Jones, victualler were recorded at the establishment in the early 1800s, when the inn also served as the post office. From the surviving documentation it appears that in 1812, the **King's Arms** was opposite the town gaol at the top of Monnow Street, but at a later date it was replaced by another **King's Arms**, which was licensed to John Barlow in 1822, William Mills in 1830, Enoch Jones in 1831, Samuel Beach in 1842, and Edward Jones in 1859. All this was before James Phillips arrived on the scene. He was the landlord who was in trouble in 1881 when he refused to admit a constable. The confrontation must have been settled for Phillips was succeeded by various landlords until the pub closed in the late 1920s.

Somewhere between the later and earlier **King's Arms** was the **Boar's Head**, another inn dating from the late 18th century, which was licensed to Matthew Wilde in 1822 when the carriers William and George North were next door. Matthew stayed at his inn until the mortgagees auctioned the 'Old-Established & Well-Accustomed Public House called the Boar's Head Inn' in 1863. Although the inn may have been in financial difficulty, it continued to trade until the 1870s when Miss Sarah Roberts was the landlady.

The next former pub on the west side of Monnow Street was the **White Lion**, situated before the entrance to Nailer's Lane. It was kept by John Rees during the first half of the 19th century after which it closed its doors.

Beyond Nailer's Lane, where the blacksmiths' were sited, is a small, narrow building, which in 2005 displayed a licence over the doorway, but lacked a name and a pub sign (see page 56). It is said to be the **Henry Fifth**, run by Richard Hughes in 1831 before he became a wine and spirit merchant in Monnow Street. No further records survive until 1881 when the **King Henry Fifth** was granted a licence, and from thereon it may have continued as a beer house or wine shop. The ancient cellars are recorded in the Monmouth Cellar Survey of 1988. Since 2005 this tiny pub has been refurbished and is now known as the **Gloucestershire House**.

Two or maybe three 18th-century inns traded at the top of Monnow Street opposite the entrance to St. John's Street. There was certainly the **Star and Garter**, kept by John Spinget in 1759 and the **Green Dragon**, formerly 'three messuages joined together' which became the **Fountain** in the mid-18th century. It is understood by Davies and Kissack that a **Swan and Falcon** stood nearby, but at the time of writing there is no evidence to support this claim. The Fountain was the meeting place of the Friendly Society of Tradesmen and Others in the early 1800s, probably under the

Licensed to sell BEERS, WINES & SPIRITS on or off the Premises
Licensees.....

Left and below: The Henry Fifth, with the enigmatic sign in 2005.
Right: The inn has reopened as the Gloucestershire House (see previous page)

management of Benjamin Green who was still there in 1842. The **Fountain** was advertised by a new landlord in the *Monmouthshire Gazette* of 1851 as follows:

> W. Waites respectfully announces to the Public that he has taken to the above Inn, which he intends to conduct with the regard for comfort and economy as will secure to him their support and patronage. Choice wines and spirits of superior quality. Well-aired beds. Good accommodation for horses.

Despite these promises the **Fountain** appears to have closed for a while until reopening in the 1880s. However, with Waites's emphasis on 'choice wines and spirits' the premises may well have served as one of the wine and spirit merchants in Monnow Street throughout the recorded period. From 1884 to 1937 Albert Preece, followed by Leonard Arthur,

The one-time Druid's Head in 2005

kept the **Fountain**, but it eventually succumbed to the dwindling trade and has since closed.

On the east side of Monnow Street, St. John's Street leads towards Glendower Street and from there to Chippenhamgate Street, where at least two former pubs existed. These were the **Globe** and the **Druid's Head**, but another two called the **Fortune** and the **Mermaid** were also in the area.

Although an entry of 1771 records the burial of 'old Mary Evans of the Globe', no further references to the inn occur until 1862 when William Jenkins was listed as the publican. Others followed, including James Smith in 1909, when the **Globe** was tied or owned by Hall's Ox Brewery. It probably closed shortly after this date; the premises being demolished in 1963 to make way for school buildings. The **Fortune** of 1718 may have been an earlier name for the **Globe**,

The well-signed Rugby Club premises in Chippenhamgate Street was formerly the **Druid's Head**, which dates from the 18th century when it was known as the **Five Courts** – the meeting place of one of Monmouth's numerous Friendly Societies. It must have been William Beavan in 1830 who changed the name to the **Druid's Head**, although in 1835 the fives courts still existed. The pub's landlords included David Evans, who was summoned to the Exchequer of Pleas at the suit of William Wilders in 1873. During the 20th century the Alton Court Brewery, based at Ross, acquired 'All that messuage or Inn in Chippenhamgate Street Monmouth known as the Druid's Head with the outbuildings yard and land adjoining', which was taken over by West Country Breweries in 1962 and closed in 1966.

The **Mermaid** of 1680 was leased in 1769 to John Jones as a house and garden with 'Mead called Chippenham Mead and Monnow Street on all sides'. The next mention appears in 1835 when William Parry, a builder, was:

applying for a Victualling House in the house I now occupy situated in Monnow Street which I hold under his Grace the Duke of Beaufort which House has formerly been kept as an Inn or Victualling House under the sign of the Mermaid by the late William Roberts.

Maybe Parry was unsuccessful with his application, or was he successful and immediately renamed the inn as the **Builder's Arms**, an inn referred to in 19th-century election expenses.

St. John's Street was the Back Lane which, according to Heath, derived its name 'from waggons and other carriages, coming with coal or lime into the county, adopting it as the line of communication with Monnow Street, instead of passing thro' the Market place'. Residences of the 18th century on the south side of St. John's, Glendower and Chippenhamgate Streets enjoyed fine views of the Mead and, during race meetings, the large gardens were used as tennis courts, bowling greens and skittle alleys, whilst one contained the Summer House visited by Nelson during his Wye Tour of 1802.

There was also a 'small public house' which may have been the **Benefaction** of 1743 situated near the **Black Swan**, an inn that shared a complicated legal history with the adjacent **Falcon**, which once stood on the corner of St. John's Street but faced onto Monnow Street.

The **Black Swan** was an 18th-century coaching inn with limited stabling, so that on market days and at busy periods extra accommodation for horses was supplied by the following method:

> to erect upright poles, over which rafters were laid, covered with faggots, and from thence obtained the name of wood piles. Under these sheds, the farmers turned their horses loose, during their stay in town, for which accommodation they paid an halfpenny per horse. Sometimes the servant brought a small bundle of hay, with which he fed them.

In 1803, a Friendly Society took the name of the **Black Swan** and held their meetings at the inn; later, in 1822, Thomas Wood was the licensee, followed by Samuel Rowley. During the 1830s and '40s Benjamin Goodall,

J. MONNINGTON,

BLACK SWAN INN

ST. JOHN'S STREET, MONMOUTH.

Good Stabling, Well-aired Beds, and every Accommodation for Travellers.

WINES AND SPIRITS OF THE BEST QUALITY.

☞ Neat Pleasure Boats and Light Skiffs for Hire on the River Wye.

The Black Swan was advertising in 1862

58

James Haywood and William Mills were listed at the inn, before the Monnington family ran the **Black Swan** for about thirty years, advertising:

> Good Stabling, Well-aired Beds, and Accomodation for Travellers. Wines and Spirits of the Best Quality. Neat Pleasure Boats and Light Skiffs for Hire on the River Wye.

The old **Black Swan** survived into the mid-20th century under the management of several landladies including Mary Jenkins in 1937.

In 1673 an agreement was made at the 'sign of the Falcon' – an inn that once stood on the east side of Monnow Street. The **Falcon** was occupied by Rachel Harper in 1750, when the inn was partly rebuilt and became the meeting place of the active Falcon Friendly Society. At Gwent Record Office a *Catalogue of Deeds* from 1826 refers to a property in Monnow Street, which also mentions the **Falcon**, occupied by James Haywood, and the **Black Swan**, where Samuel Rowley lived. James Haywood died in 1851 and was succeeded at the **Falcon** by Arthur Hockley, but the Haywood family obviously kept an interest in the adjoining stable, for at a later date a relative was ordered 'to block up doors and windows between the stable and the Falcon Inn'. This was a few years before the inn closed in the mid-1870s.

Once the Nag's Head

On the east side of Monnow Street almost opposite Nailer's Lane was the **Nag's Head**, owned by Herbert Aubrey and occupied by Abell Wantner in 1713, and kept by Edward Harris, a butcher, in 1750. From 1822 William Giles and his family took over the licence until 1854, when James Pembridge agreed to take over the lease and the 'stock furniture fixtures utensils and implements in trade' for 'such a sum as the same shall be valued and agreed'; to pay twenty pounds for 'good will', and be 'paid ten pounds towards the necessary repairs of said premises' by the outgoing landlord, Arthur Hockley. James stayed at the **Nag's Head** until 1871 after which it was kept by Aquila Palmer followed by Alfred Sutton in the 1880s before finally closing as an inn.

Adjoining the **Nag's Head** was a 'messuage and tenement called the Holy Lamb now in the tenure of William Greene' in 1713. The premises, with 'one stable, backside and garden' was occupied by Anthony Jones, a maltster, in 1750. After the marriage of his daughter, Gwenlian, to the owner of the property, the **Holy Lamb** appears to have closed.

The **Butchers' Arms** was open within living memory at 50 Monnow Street. It had already been established in the late 18th century as a 'sporting' inn associated with cock-fighting and bare-knuckle boxing. An advertisement in the *Gloucestershire Journal* in 1772 announced:

BUTCHERS' ARMS HOTEL
The Old-Established Family and Market House.

TELEPHONE 67

Best Accommodation for Tourists and others

Garage and Stabling for 40 Horses. Open & Closed Cars.

Motor Hearses, etc., for Funeral Work

Proprietor - CHAS. PREECE

CATERING for LARGE or SMALL PARTIES

MONNOW ST. - - MONMOUTH

A 1923 advertisement for the Butchers' Arms

A cock-match to be fought at The Butcher's Arms in Monmouth between the Gentlemen of Herefordshire and Monmouthshire to weigh 31 cocks on each side – on the Main – for two guineas a Battle and 40 the odd battle, and 20 for Byes for one guinea a battle; to weigh on Monday the 25th April and fight the three following days. Richard King and Francis Morgan, Feeders. An Ordinary every day at the Cocking House.

It is possible that the same 'gentlemen' of Monmouth continued this cruel sport at the New Inn at Lydbrook the following year – an event also reported in the *Gloucestershire Journal* (see *Pubs of the Royal Forest of Dean*).

In 1822 James Collins applied for the licence of the **Butchers' Arms**, but Thomas Wood then Susannah Wood kept the pub until 1839 when Susannah held a farewell dinner. Her successor was Mr. J. Harper, who was unsuccessful as a landlord, although a Friendly Society met there between 1842 and 1852. The next name listed at the inn is Thomas Wilkes, who also worked as a veterinary surgeon and was helped by Ann Wilkes until around 1880. The Laws family were then followed by Charles Preece who, despite offering 'Stabling for 40 Horses', welcomed 'Open & Closed Cars' to be parked in his 'Garage' during the 1920s and '30s.

Situated between the **Butcher's Arms** and Cornwall House was the **Plough** of the 18th century, which was converted into the laundry and kitchen of Cornwall House in 1756.

In 1887 an ostler from the **Butchers' Arms** was charged with being drunk in charge of a horse and trap – one of numerous offences associated with drunk and disorderly behaviour, dangerous driving (of horses) and offensive language. Earlier, in 1840, a story related in *The Pubs of Ross and South Herefordshire* follows the pub crawl of a man who died in Monmouth Police Station. He had walked from St. Weonards in Herefordshire, and on his way consumed three pints of ale in Herefordshire pubs before drinking another pint at the **Mason's Cross**, five pints at the **Nag's Head** in Monnow Street and large quantities of rum at the **Market Tavern**.

Offences relating to the consumption of alcohol and being in charge of a vehicle are of long standing. Thus, between 1853 and 1856 the *Merlin* newspaper and the local bench recorded a collection of incidents including: 'William Freeman, a smith, charged with indecent conduct, with assaulting the police, and with being at the time drunk'. He was convicted and paid a fine of 10s. and costs'. In 1854 Timothy Lewis of Wolverhampton was charged with having left his waggon in Monnow Street 'longer than required for unloading', so he was probably enjoying a drink at one of the local inns. John Watkins, beer house keeper in Monmouth, was charged 'with having on Sunday, the 3rd inst., kept his house open for the sale of beer, at an illegal hour'. The case was dismissed as the 'only man who had had beer was a traveller from Joyford'. The same year, William Jenkins from Dewchurch in Herefordshire collapsed and died after drinking at the **Vine Tree**.

Towards the southern end of Monnow Street, on the east side, was the **Borough Arms**, easily recognisable by its old sign bearing the name of 'The Borough Pharmacy'. It was originally called the **Ropemakers Arms**, when James Watkins, a rope maker and flax dresser, licensed the pub in 1822. John

Beavan took over the lease of the 'messuage called the Ropemakers in Monnow Street and cider house or ware room', and was later followed by Nelson Williams, William Bigham and finally in 1895 by Aquila Palmer who renamed it the **Borough Arms**. Before the pub closed it was taken over by

The Borough Arms is now a pharmacy

61

Ansells Brewery, and when Mr. A.G. Matthews was the landlord in 1988 photographs of the beer cellars were featured in the *Monmouth Cellar Survey* compiled by E. Steggles – a copy of which is available at the Nelson Museum.

The **Robin Hood** is housed in one of Monmouth's oldest buildings and cannot be missed at the bottom of Monnow Street. Its restored doorway dates from the 16th century and its interior features carved beams and timber partitions of the late 17th century. In the past, before catholic tolerance, a room was used to say mass, until a Roman Catholic church was built by the landlord, Michael Watkins, in 1792. The **Robin Hood** sign is understood to be of 18th-century origin and featured:

> Walk in kind sirs, my ale is good,
> and take a pot with Robin Hood;
> If Robin Hood is not at home
> Pray take a pot with Little John

The Pollards ran the **Robin Hood** through the 1820s and '30s, and at the turn of the century Edward Lewis was the landlord. A Miss Violet Lewis, presumably his daughter, was appointed as caretaker of Monnow Gate in 1902. During the 20th century the Alton Court Brewery from Ross-on-Wye acquired the premises, which was sold to West Country Breweries in 1962 as 'All That messuage or Inn in Monnow Street Monmouth known as the Robin Hood Inn with the outbuildings yard and land thereto adjoining and belonging'. The **Robin Hood** was then taken over by Whitbread and in the 1970s was offering 'Modern Comfort, Old World Charm, Delightful Bar

The Robin Hood in 2005

Meals and Snacks, Wide Range Bar Stock'. These services have extended into the 21st century.

The remaining named pubs in Monnow Street are at sites that have not so far been identified. There was the **British Workman** of 1880, the **Loyal Welshman**, mentioned in a marriage settlement of 1758 when talking of 'a newly erected messuage dwelling house situated in or near Monnow Street, on the site of the Loyal Welshman now pulled down'. In 1822 the **Smith's Arms** was licensed to William Howells – probably related to the family of blacksmiths and nail makers of that period, and finally the **Crown and Anchor** – a short-lived 19th-century beer house with a name suggesting a riverside site.

In Monnow Street and Chippenhamgate Street there were a few beer retailers that traded without any obvious pub sign. Numerous malt houses existed, including the 'backside malthouse stable etc.' of 1718 and the 'Messuage where Timothy Morse formerly dwelt with malthouse, garden, yard and backside', of 1792. Towards the end of the 19th century the malt-sters business expanded as is shown by William Hyam's advertisement in 1871 where he worked as a 'corn, seed, flour and hop merchant, maltsters, soda water manufacturer'. His family's mineral water, manufactured in Glendower Street, was appreciated by the Duke of Beaufort. John Roberts had erected a brewery in Monnow Street by 1866, when curiously the room above was used as a Primitive Methodist Chapel. In 1871, Henry Tippins was established as a 'brewer, wholesale and retail wine and spirit merchant, agent for Burton beers and Dublin stout' at number 3 Monnow Street. Other wine and spirit merchants were John Masters and Mrs. Mary Court in 1862, the Misses Jones of 1895, and Lloyd and Yorath Brewery's off-licence.

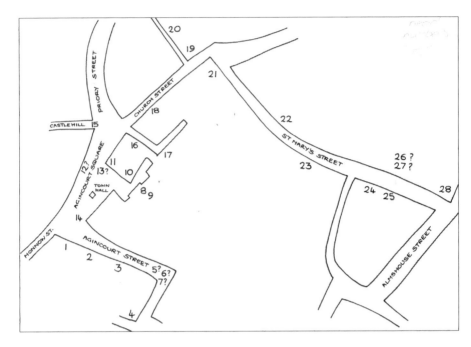

1. **King's Head**
2. Eight Bells/Agincourt
3. Red Streak Tree
4. Squirrel/Greyhound
5. Coach & Horses
6. Royal Arms
7. Plow Ale House
8. Beaufort Arms
9. Beaufort Arms Tap
10. Bull / Black Bull
11. **Wine Vaults/Punch House**
12. Duke of Wellington /
    Reformer's Tavern / Barrel
13. Bear?
14. Jolly Postboy
15. King & Queen

16. Cross Keys Inn
17. Golden Ball
18. Red Lion
19. Ye Blew Bell/Bell
20. Ye George
21. Angel
22. **Malt House**
23. Black Lion
24. Crown/Crown & Sceptre
25. Carpenter's Arms
26. Harp Inn
27. Lamb
28. Gloucestershire House

Bold open in 2007

MONMOUTH – Chapter 5: Agincourt Square, Church Street
& St. Mary's Street

CHAPTER FIVE

Monmouth:
AGINCOURT SQUARE, CHURCH STREET & ST. MARY'S STREET

Agincourt Square was originally known as the Market Place until around 1830; today, with the adjoining streets, it forms the heart of Monmouth. In the square an open market is still held each Friday, with its colourful array of stalls selling a variety of goods from jam to jewellery. Agincourt Street is of a later date, but Church Street, known earlier as Butcher's Row, and St. Mary's Street, enjoy a long history of occupation. All the horse-drawn coaches and waggons travelling from Ross and London to South Wales had to negotiate the narrow Church Street before the construction of Priory Street in 1837.

In 1804, Heath, the reliable Monmouth antiquarian, wrote:

> Church Street was originally a mere thoroughfare, scarcely wide enough to admit a loaded waggon to pass through it. Every door had its pent-house, with its seat under it, which afforded the opportunity to inquisitive minds of watching their neighbour's business, instead of attending to their own. When Sir John Stepney, Baronet, was elected M.P. for the borough, it was altered and improved at his expence; in compliment to whom it was as frequently called Stepney Street.

He added that St. Mary's Street 'derives its name from the Mother of Saints, to whom the parish church is dedicated'.

Nowadays Agincourt Square and the pedestrianised Church Street form the busy centre of Monmouth for visitors to admire the statues of Henry V and Charles Rolls, the Shire Hall, and the interesting shops and cafés. In the past plentiful pubs lined the streets and the square, which led to the following traditional rhyme:

A gin court here,
a gin court there,
no wonder they call it
Agincourt Square.

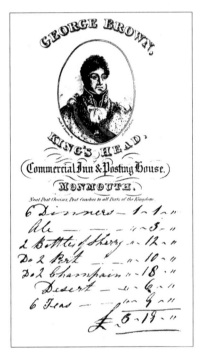

Dinner and tea for six people at the King's Head in 1830

This chapter covers an area in Monmouth where there were 15 pubs in 1835, six in 1937, but reduced to only two in 2005 although there are some licensed cafés and restaurants.

From Agincourt Square the street of the same name is dominated by the extensive buildings of the **King's Head**, a Wetherspoon's family pub of the 21st century, but with a long history dating from the mid-17th century. This was when Richard Ballard kept the inn and erected a plaster cast in memory of Charles I, who reputedly visited the inn in 1645 when he was staying at Raglan. During the 18th century the **King's Head** became one of the principal coaching inns of Monmouth. Here important celebrations were held, including one held for the corporation in 1799 when large amounts of porter, cider, port, sherry, punch, toddy and wine was consumed. Charles Heath in 1804 wrote:

Before the erection of the Beaufort Arms, the King's Head was the principal inn in the borough, kept at the time by Mrs. Bayliss, after which it was held by the late Mr. William Rogers; who being a spirited character, very much improved its accommodations. On his retiring from business, it was taken by Mr. Thomas Webbe; who was succeeded by Mr. Thomas Hart, and he by Mr. James Baker, after whose resignation it was further improved by the proprietor (J.T.Bourne, esq.) and is now occupied by Mr. Crutchley.

In 1822 Thomas Stratford was the licensee, followed by George Brown who appears to have run into debt and sold his 'Goods and Chattels' to raise £893 10s 11d. in 1828, although he was still recorded at the establishment at a later date. The inventory of the sale in 1828 records an inn containing many bedrooms with four-post and tent bedsteads, several reception rooms, a coffee room, a commercial room, a ballroom, tap room, servants' room, a brewhouse with tubs and furnaces, a kitchen, larder and pantry containing massive sets of of dinner plates and soup bowls, a post boys' room, gig house, stables, granary, a bar and a cellar full of hogsheads, beer casks, soda and ginger beer bottles, 21 gallons of brandy, 25 of rum, 32 of gin, 8 of whisky, 32 of sherry, 27 of port and cider, 30 of cider, and casks of vinegar and oil.

Shortly after Mr. Brown's departure, John Robertson took over the **King's Head** and in 1840 he also sold the contents which included 16 coach horses. Horses were essential to draw the coaches, which had names such as *Hero*, *Rapid*, *Times*, the *White Lion* and the *Tourist* in 1850 when John Webb was the proprietor. Coaching continued as an important business under the management of Alfred Bennett and John Thomas who offered 'Ladies Coffee and Drawing Rooms, Good Billiard Room, Stabling, Photographic Dark Room free, Omnibus to All Trains' at his 'Hotel and Posting House'.

New Coach

TO

LONDON,

THE

PAUL PRY

Through Ross, Gloucester, Cheltenham, and Oxford, from the

King's Head Hotel, Monmouth,

Every Day at One, (Sundays excepted.)—Leaves the Blossoms' Inn, Lawrence Lane, London, at Six in the Evening, and arrives in Monmouth by Twelve the following Day.

ROBERTSON & Co. Proprietors

THE

KING'S HEAD HOTEL,

MONMOUTH,

Is replete with every convenience, both as a Family and Commercial Hotel.

Tourists will find every Accommodation at Moderate Charges.

THE "TIMES" COACH

LEAVES THE ABOVE HOTEL,

Every Morning, (Sundays excepted,)

At Twenty Minutes before Nine precisely,

THROUGH WHITCHURCH AND PENCRAIG,

Arriving at

BARRETT'S HOTEL, & THE RAILWAY STATION,

R O S S,

At Ten o'Clock, in time for the First, Second and Third-class Trains to

LONDON, HEREFORD, & GLOUCESTER.

Returning : leaves the Station and Barretts Hotel, after the arrival of the 4.5 P.M. Trains from London, Hereford and Gloucester, arriving in Monmouth at 5.40.

Coaches from the King's Head in the mid-19th century before and after Ross station opened

King's Head advertisements:
Top: 1859, Middle: 1862, Bottom 1895

68

Before the motor car – scenes outside the King's Head about 1900

The local beauty spots were emphasised in this 1905 advertisement

King's Head Hotel

AGINCOURT SQUARE

A picturesque Hotel, in popular legend associated with Charles Stuart, now well-equipped with modern amenities and service. The best centre for a lovely District.

Telephone Monmouth 17.   Garage.

TRUST HOUSES LIMITED

After the Second World War the King's Head, the Beaufort and the Angel all became Trust Houses

The King's Head in 2005

At the beginning of the 20th century A.E. Hyam took over the hotel and offered 'Posting and Livery Stables, Lock-Up Loose Boxes' together with 'Good Cycle and Motor Accommodation'. It was later purchased by Trust Houses Ltd. who published a series of leaflets on the history of their hotels entitled *The Tales of Old Inns*. The one covering the **King's Head** referred to the possible visit of Charles I and the plaster cast that by tradition was placed in a certain position so that the vain king could admire his own effigy while seated in his favourite place. In the 1970s the hotel was:

> modernised to meet the needs of the 20th-century traveller ... an ideal centre for exploring the Wye Valley and Border area. All rooms with private facilities, radio, telephone and colour TV.

However, all was not well, and by the end of the century the hotel stood empty and derelict for a while, until it was taken over by Wetherspoons as 'a no nonsense family pub. Great prices for bottled beer and food, non-smoking areas, no music, beer garden and a family room'.

The one time Agincourt in 2005

Almost next to the **King's Head** is the site of the **Eight Bells** kept by Richard Green throughout the 1820s and '30s when a Female Friendly Society met there. In 1842 Thomas Pritchard was innkeeper before Thomas Weaver served as the last landlord in 1859. The sign of the **Eight Bells** suggests the meeting place of the bell ringers, who at that time were paid in ale. It is understood that the **Agincourt** of 1884 stood on the same site, and traded for around 100 years before closing – its sign still being visible.

In 1885 a party of guests staying at the **Agincourt** visited the Forest of Dean to investigate the Buckstone, a huge rocking stone. John Stratford wrote the story in *The Wye Tour* published in 1895:

A party of six men – five belonging to a London theatrical company, who had performed at the Borough Court on the two previous evenings, and the other Mr. Philpotts, of the Agincourt Inn, Monmouth, with whom the company had been staying – went, like any other casual visitor, to see the stone. Two of the number clambered to the top, as is generally done by some one or more of every party of tourists, thouth the feat was by no means an easy one. While on the summit, the others commenced pushing, to see if the stone, so alleged, really would rock. Suddenly they were surprised to see the large mass of conglomorate turn half round and next moment topple over down the hill, the two men on the top having only just time to jump off and save themselves from being crushed, as they probably would have been beneath its weight. It was broken into three pieces, which lodged about 200 feet below the place where it had stood for centuries, but innumerable fragments were scattered about, and soon became prey to the thousands of people who were at once attracted to the spot and desired to retain a memento of the Buckstone.

Since then the stone has been cemented together.

Two former Monmouth pubs:
Top: The Red Streak Tree
Bottom: The Greyhound

The **Red Streak Tree** once stood on the south side of Agincourt Street. It was licensed to William Richards in 1822, but its name suggests an earlier establishment named after the Redstreak cider apple grown by Lord Scudamore at Holme Lacy in Herefordshire shortly after the Civil War. The **Red Streak Tree** continued to flourish during the 19th century until it closed around 1875.

At the southern corner of Agincourt Street is a building that is easily recognised as a former pub. It was recorded in 1818 as 'All that messuage, tenement or dwelling house now called the Squirrel with the Brewhouse and appurtenances thereto belonging formerly in the tenure of William Morgan and also all those two stables adjoining'. The pub was still known as the **Squirrel** in 1822 when James Waters was the licensee, but by 1831 it had been renamed the **Greyhound**. It was then kept by Richard Wilks who was robbed of £7 10s. One of his lodgers, a man called Clark, was suspected of the crime, but when taken to court the case was dismissed due to insufficient evidence. Unfortunately Clark was still suspected and was nearly drowned in the river by being ducked by a team of bargemen hoping for a confession. A succession of publicans followed Wilks until the **Greyhound** closed in 1885.

Three other pubs were recorded in Agincourt Street: the **Coach and Horses**, briefly kept by George Humphries in the 1860s; the **Royal Arms** of 1871 kept by Hannah Andrews; and the **Plow Ale House** of 1723.

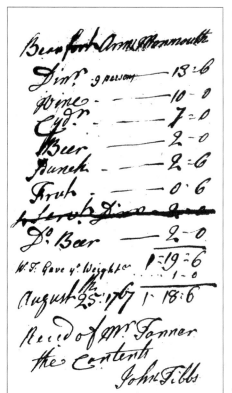

Left: Dinner for nine people at the Beaufort Hotel in 1767

Above: A more formal bill from 1792

In Agincourt Square the former **Beaufort Arms** cannot be missed, as its name is still displayed across the building which has recently been converted into a complex of shops and apartments. The **Beaufort** was another of Monmouth's important coaching inns dating from the early 18th century. According to Heath it was converted by John Tibbs from two small tenements and a fives court. The inn took its name from the former owner of the property, and Tibbs added to its attractions by laying out pleasure gardens and river walks in Vauxhall, which were reached by a

LOT NINETEEN.

(Coloured Pink on Plan and the Cellars shown Green.)

AN IMPORTANT FREEHOLD PROPERTY,

Situate in the centre of the County Town of Monmouth, and known as the

"BEAUFORT ARMS" HOTEL,

WITH THE

BEAUFORT TAP

ADJOINING.

Covering an area of about **3,284 Square Yards**, approached from Agincourt Square by the Shire Hall or County Assize Courts, and from Agincourt Street at the side.

The Hotel is entered by Covered Way, with Handsome Double Gates to enclose the Yard at night. Glazed Folding Doors open to the Public Entrance, Bar, Bar Parlour, Commercial Room, 21 ft. by 19 ft. 6 in., Coffee Room, panelled in Mahogany, Lavatory, and Three Cellars under.

In the Wing are

Market Room, 23 ft. 6 in. by 22 ft., with Side Entrance, Kitchen, 33 ft. 9 ins. by 19 ft. 6 ins., Larder, Kitchen, Yard giving access to Scullery, Wash House, Coal and Wood Sheds, Meat Larder and Bottle Stores, and a

Seven-Roomed Cottage

On the right of Covered Entrance adjoining Shire Hall, Manager's Office, Luggage Room, and Boot's Office, with Cellars, which are under part of the Shire Hall belonging to the Corporation.

ON THE FIRST FLOOR approached by Easy Stairs from Entrance Hall, are:—

GRAND BALL ROOM
50 ft. by 24 ft. 6 ins.,

With raised Orchestra Stand at end, and Polished Oak Floor, Three Sitting Rooms, spacious cupboards and Wine Room Six Bed Rooms, W.C., and Waiter's Pantry.

ON THE SECOND FLOOR—Eleven Bed Rooms, Two Housemaids' Closet with Sink, Linen Press and W.C.

ON THE THIRD FLOOR—Fourteen Bed Rooms.

Surrounding a Cobble Paved Yard is

BILLIARD ROOM,
26 ft. 6 ins. by 21 ft. 9 ins., with Stone Staircase.

Also the following Stable and Coach House Premises.

Four Bay Carriage Shed, Four Stall Stable, Loose Box, Lofts, Hay Room, and Saddle Room.

Four Closed Coach Houses, Chaff Cutting Room, and extensive Corn Stores.

In another Yard at Side are

STABLE STANDING SIXTEEN HORSES, THREE FOUR-HORSE STABLES, THREE LOOSE BOXES, STABLE OF FOUR STALLS AND TWO LOOSE BOXES. A LOOSE BOX AND

GARDEN WITH GREENHOUSE

THE

BEAUFORT TAP

Adjoins, but is entirely separated from the Hotel; has separate approach and contains Bar, Bar Parlour, Kitchen, Back Kitchen, Three Bed Rooms, Lumber Attic and Cellar. This holds a separate license, and is sub-let to Mrs. THOMAS, at a Rent of **£18** a Year.

The whole of the forgoing being let on a Yearly Tenancy from 2nd February to the Monmouth Hotel Company, at a rent of **£100** per Annum. Tenants pay Land Tax, **£4 2s. 8d.**

The Tithe, if any, belonging to the MARQUIS OF WORCESTER, is included in the Sale.

Sale of the Beaufort Arms in 1899

Monmouth, Ross, and Gloucester.

THE Public are respectfully informed that on and after MONDAY, the 11th inst.,

The "Mazeppa" Fast Coach,

Will leave the BEAUFORT ARMS and KING'S HEAD HOTELS, MONMOUTH, every Morning, Sundays excepted, at a Quarter before Seven ; passing through Ross and arriving in Gloucester at Ten, in time for the Parliamentary Cheap Train that leaves the Station at 27 minutes past 10.

Fares throughout to London 14s. 7d.

On its return it will leave the Station at Half-past Four, and Heath's Office, and Bell Hotel, Five minutes afterwards, immediately after the arrival of Trains from London, Manchester, Liverpool, and Bristol.

This Coach affords an accommodation long desired as it is the only conveyance that leaves Monmouth in time for the Parliamentary Train, by which Passengers can reach any station for 1d. per mile.

June 5th.   BARRETT & CO., Proprietors

MONMOUTH.

The "Beaufort Arms" Hotel,
CONDUCTED BY THE

MONMOUTH HOTEL COMPANY, LIMITED,

Affords First-class Accommodation on Moderate Terms.

☞ Servants charged in the Bill. Families supplied with Wine, Spirits, &c., at Wholesale Prices.

POSTING IN ALL ITS BRANCHES.

Coaches to and from Ross daily. Omnibuses to meet each Train.

Left: The Mazeppa *coach ensured that the citizens of Monmouth could catch the 'Parliamentary Cheap train' from Gloucester to London*

Above: The Beaufort Arms Hotel was taken over by the Monmouth Hotel Co. about 1860

Coaches leaving the Beaufort Arms Hotel about 1905

BEAUFORT : ARMS : HOTEL,

MONMOUTH.

FRANK SWIFT

Has received instructions from PERCY B. TIMINGS. Esq., the Receiver for the Debenture Holder, to Sell by Auction, on the Premises,

On FRIDAY, JUNE 22nd, 1917,

At TWO o'clock p.m. precisely, subject to Conditions to be then produced (unless previously disposed of by private treaty)—**THE IMPORTANT**

Freehold Property

consisting of the **FULLY-LICENSED**

FAMILY AND COMMERCIAL HOTEL,

**Known as THE BEAUFORT ARMS HOTEL,
AGINCOURT SQUARE, MONMOUTH,**

Together with the whole of the EXCELLENT FIXTURES, FITTINGS, HOTEL FURNITURE, VEHICLES, and General Effects (other than consumable stock),

IN ONE LOT AS A GOING CONCERN.

The accommodation includes :—Twenty-six Bedrooms, Two Bathrooms, Private Sitting Rooms, Coffee Room, Drawing Room, Commercial Room, Spacious Banqueting Room, with alcove ; Entrance Hall, Smoke Room, Bar, Bar Parlour, Billiard Room, Market Room, Extensive Kitchens, Sculleries, Larders, Service Room, Stores and Cellaring, Lavatories, etc., etc. Outside there is Large Yard, with stabling for about forty horses, Coach-house, Lofts, Garage, Engine House, and walled-in Garden.

Area 3,177 Square Yards or thereabouts.

The Hotel is fitted with electric light, electric bells and hot and cold water.

POSSESSION ON COMPLETION OF PURCHASE.

The Inventory of Effects can be inspected at the Auctioneers' Offices, Seven days previous to the Sale.

NOTE.—The Beaufort Arms Hotel is the leading Hotel in Monmouth, being situate in the very centre of the town, adjoining the Shire Hall and Market Place.

For particulars apply to Messrs. FORSYTH, BETTINSON & CO., Solicitors, 36, Cannon Street ; PERCY B. TIMINGS, Esq., Chartered Accountant, 47, Temple Row ; or the AUCTIONEER, 1, Waterloo Street, all of Birmingham.

Sale of the Beaufort Arms in 1917

78

The Beaufort was one of the Monmouth hotels taken over by Trust Houses

79

The Beaufort Arms still makes use of its coach entry, but is now a shopping mews

footbridge over the Monnow. The **Beaufort** became the main place to stay, and was visited by the Hon. John Byng in 1781. In his *Torrington Diaries* he wrote:

arriv'd at the Beaufort Arms, Monmouth, this evening, rather tired, (owing more to weak nerves than to any other cause), and am now sitting in a mean room at the back of a bad inn; which may be the best here. The stables are new and good, that's a comfort; for if my horse does not fare and sleep well, well there wou'd be an end of my travell.

In the early 1800s John Watkins kept the **Beaufort Arms** and must have been responsible for entertaining Lord Nelson and his party when they visited in 1802. Watkins was followed by Thomas Avery, who managed the inn for a lengthy period when coaches ran to London on the *Royal Mail* and the *Mazeppa*; to Brecon on the *Nimrod*; and to Bristol on the *White Lion*. The fare to London was 15s. outside or 30s. inside the coach for a journey that took 15 hours.

From around 1860 the **Beaufort** was run by the Monmouth Hotel Company who advertised their establishment as the 'Hotel & Posting House for Families & Tourists & Commercial Gentlemen' before the Beaufort Estate sold the premises in 1899 (page 76). There was also a Wine and Spirit Merchants open there in 1884, and by 1905 the hotel had 'Electric Light, Baths, Posting, Motor Garage, Table D'Hote'. The hotel was advertised for sale in 1917 with its 26 bedrooms, sitting rooms, coffee, drawing and commercial rooms, spacious banqueting hall, bars, billiard room, cellaring and stabling for 40 horses. It appears to have remained under the management of the Monmouth Hotel Company until it was acquired by Trust Houses Ltd., who boasted 'The Best Service at Moderate Tariffs'. The hotel survived into the late 1970s, but offering only restaurant meals, bar snacks and conference facilities was appparently not sufficient and it eventually closed.

Adjacent to the **Beaufort Arms** was the **Beaufort Arms Tap** opened by J.H. Hurd in 1864. He served foreign spirits, Allsopp's pure Burton Ale at 5d. a Quart, tea, coffee, chops and steak. In the 1890s, when Elija Thomas ran the **Tap**, it was used by the grooms, ostlers and servants from the hotel. Charles Curtis in 1910 was the last known publican of the **Tap**, which has since been demolished.

On the east side of Agincourt Square and opposite the Shire Hall was the **Black Bull** of the 18th century, which became simply the **Bull**

The Beaufort Arms Tap about 1890

Harry and Mary Dowson
welcome you to

The Bull Inn

AGINCOURT SQUARE, MONMOUTH

Telephone : 2226

A VARIETY OF SNACKS AT BAR
OVERNIGHT ACCOMMODATION
GOOD CAR PARKING FACILITIES

A FRIENDLY PUB WITH GOOD BEER
(A Free House)

A 1970s advertisement for the Bull, before it became part of the Punch House

The Monmouth Wine & Spirit Offices

when licensed to Charles Tudor in 1822. Apart from the inn being kept by members of the same Upstill family from the 1850s to the 1880s and hosting meetings of a friendly society, no other known events took place there. At a later date it was incorporated into the **Punch House**.

The existing **Punch House** is thriving, with

The Punch House – Top: about 1896, Bottom: 2005

82

their customers enjoying wine, beer and pub grub. It was originally established as the **Wine Vaults** and licensed to John Powell in 1822, but by 1831 it was known as the **Punch House**. It appears to have traded as a wine and spirit merchants by the Powell family until at least 1895. It re-appeared again as the **Punch House Hotel** in 1939 with the following advertisement: 'The noted house for Draught Bass – Best English Steaks – Mixed Grills – Luncheons – Teas – Suppers – Bed and Breakfast'. The proprietor was R.C. Seymour, who had converted his previous wine and spirit business into an hotel.

On the west side of the square, and now lost in a line of buildings, was the **Barrel** which kept by John Pembridge in 1884 before closing in 1907. Previously it had been known as the **Duke of Wellington** until about 1830 when the Hughes family altered its name, in sympathy with political change, to the **Reformer's Tavern**.

At an unknown site in the market square there was a large inn known as the **Bear** in 1610, when the landlord was John Mason. However, the last known reference to the old inn is in a lease of 1703 which mentions 'formerly lands belonging to the Beare Inn now in possession of Henry Barnes of the said Towne, gent'. In the mid-1800s there was also an inn known as the **Jolly Postboy**.

From the east side of Agincourt Square a lane called Castle Hill leads up to the ruins of Monmouth Castle and Great Castle House. The castle dates from *c.*1068 as a timber structure, being rebuilt in stone in the 12th century. The castle is worth a visit to enjoy the views and admire the great 14th-century tower which claims to

The one-time Red Lion in 2005

83

be the birthplace of Henry V in 1387. The adjoining Great Castle House, which is an impressive building built from the ruins in 1673, is the headquarters of the Royal Monmouthshire Royal Engineers and contains the joint Castle and Regimental Museum. Nearby is the site of a long-forgotten inn called the **King and Queen**, mentioned in 1698.

Between the former **Beaufort Arms** and the existing **Punch House**, a passageway called the Barton and another once known as Cross Keys Lane linked the square with Church Street. On the west side there was the **Cross Keys Inn**, established in the 18th century. It apparently had somewhat of a chequered history – in 1819 the landlord was fined for allowing Charles Heath's servant to gamble in the pub; in 1836 the mayor was found 'dead drunk outside the steps of the Cross Keys Inn'; and in 1863 a drunken man fell down the stairs to his death. These incidents, recorded by Davies and Kissack, probably occurred during the occupancy of James Hayward, Thomas Probert, and John Watkins as licensees before the inn finally closed.

On the opposite side of the lane was the former **Golden Ball**, also established in the 18th century, and kept by Mary Green, John Morgan and John Drew. Drew was the longest serving landlord, being there from 1842 until the 1860s when the inn was closed.

Church Street is now a pedestrianised thoroughfare leading from Agincourt Square to the parish church. It is dedicated to St. Mary and was originally a priory church which was rebuilt in 1735 and 1882. Only two pubs have been recorded in Church Street, one being the **Red Lion** of the 17th century, mentioned in a marriage settlement dated 1744 as the:

Messuage where John Betham the elder dwelt, now in possession of Samuel Stonehouse, Chandler and the other messuage adjoining now in possession of William Jarvis, Baker, with the two Stables and one Garden belonging which were formerly one dwelling house called the Red Lyon.

In 1787 it was referred to as 'the Old Inn, now Red Lion and now converted into a private house'.

The other pub was known by the sign of **Ye Blew Bell** in 1677 and in 1744 was a:

messuage called the Blue Bell where Elizabeth Williams did formerly live and now where Michael and Henry Humphreys dwell with the Stables, Courts, Yards and Gardens in Butcher Row [Church Street].

The **Blue Bell** was licensed to Ann Howe in 1822, William Watkins in 1831 and Thomas Wilkes in 1835. He was still there in 1839 when the *Beacon* newspaper reported that Vincent Barnes attempted to hold a Chartist meeting at the **Bell**, but the Town Crier would not announce the meeting.

After the occupancy of Thomas Wilkes the **Bell** became a theatre and the site has since been reused as the cinema.

Before the construction of Priory Street in 1837, Church Street was the main thoroughfare through the town. An incident occurred at an unknown date which probably speeded up the building of the new road – it is related by Keith Kissack in *Monmouth and its Buildings:*

> Mrs. Syner, a gingerbread maker, was closing her shutters in Church Street one evening as the Liverpool mail coach went through at full gallop. Her apron strings became caught in the harness of one of the leading horses and she was dragged almost to the Dixton Gate before the coachman could stop. He got down, thinking she might be dead, but Mrs. Syner rose to her feet, grabbed his whip, knocked out some of his teeth with the handle, and marched off to her shop to begin organising a petition for a by-pass to get the coaches out of Church Street.

The **Bell Inn** gave its name to Bell Lane, otherwise known as Inch Lane being a narrow passageway. By tradition it is said that these passageways were designed for those who drank too much and needed to feel their way around the town and its numerous drinking dens! **Ye George** of 1716, occupied by John Phillips, was situated in Inch Lane, the last licensee being George Carver in 1822. Given its size, it is difficult to imagine that George Tippins was malting in 1859 and Henry Tippins was brewing in 1871 at the Monmouth Steam Brewery Company, both situated in the narrow Inch Lane, before moving their business into St. Mary's Street.

St. Mary's Street leads from the church towards the river Wye, and before 1799 the street, according to Charles Heath, was in such a neglected state 'that in the Winter or dark evenings it was difficult to pass with safety'. Heath is remembered on a memorial by the churchyard gate where he is described as 'Bookseller, Historian, Antiquarian'. He died at the age of 70 in 1831.

In the past several inns and taverns in St. Mary's Street catered for the townsfolk, travellers and traders. The most notable was the **Angel** on the west side, a site which enjoys a long documented history from medieval times. It was a workshop in the 13th century, a church brewhouse in the 16th century and an inn from around 1700. Charles Heath in 1804 wrote the following:

> The Angel Inn kept by Mrs. Pugh, has long been a house of great respectability, and frequented by the mercantile travellers of the kingdom, whose business connects them with the trading part of the borough, – and is but justice to add, that her kind attentions to her guests, has long secured her the highest place in their good opinion.

Heath adds some interesting notes about the opposite side of the street, for which he:

P. D. MADDOX,
WINE AND SPIRIT MERCHANT,
"ANGEL" HOTEL, MONMOUTH,

BEGS to announce that he has succeeded to the above OLD-ESTABLISHED BUSINESS, and hopes to receive an increased amount of support to that enjoyed by his predecessors, to which end his utmost endeavours will at all times be exerted.

1882.   1882.   1882.

FINEST LONDON GIN	2s. per Bottle,	12s.	per Gallon.
CHOICE IRISH WHISKY	3s.	,,	18s.	,,
SUPERIOR SCOTCH WHISKY	3s.	,,	18s.	,,
HENNESSY'S OLD COGNAC BRANDY	4s. 6d.	,,	27s.	,,
VERY OLD PINE APPLE RUM	3s.	,,	18s.	,,
SUPERIOR OLD PORT	2s. 9d.	,,	16s.	,,
FINEST PALE SHERRY	2s. 6d.	,,	15s.	,,
EXCELLENT OLD-BOTTLED CLARET	2s.	,,	24s.	per Dozen.
SPARKLING CHAMPAGNE	3s.	,,	36s.	,,

P. D. M., in drawing the attention of Private Families to these Prices, desires to remark that all his Goods are guaranteed of Genuine Quality and unsurpassed in value.

NOTE THE ADDRESS—   "ANGEL" HOTEL, MONMOUTH.

The Angel price list in 1882 when gin was 10d. per bottle

MONMOUTH.
✠ ANGEL HOTEL, ✠
(OLD ESTABLISHED.)

Families and Commercial Gentlemen will find this House replete with every comfort and moderate charges.

Spacious Ladies' Coffee Room; Private Sitting Room.
OMNIBUS PASSES THE DOOR TO MEET EVERY TRAIN.
POST HORSES AND CARRIAGES.
MARY CREEPER, Proprietress.

The Angel was 'old-established' by 1884

dates its improvement to a few individuals of the present day. The first three houses formed the Theatre, at the time under the management of Mr. J. Kemble, father of Mr. J. Kemble and Mrs. S. Siddons, – while below them was a large old building, occupied by Mr. John George, afterwards by his son William, who successfully carried on the business of corn-factors for many years. After their decease it was bought by Mr. T. Hughes, sen., and of his family purchased by Mr. John Lewis, who took down the premises, and erected on the site the present houses. The residence of Mr. Prosser, Surgeon, was a small public house, and the garden a skittle alley, kept by Thomas Marret.

Angel Hotel, Monmouth.

FAMILY AND COMMERCIAL.

HEAD QUARTERS C.T.C.   DARK=ROOM.

Monmouth is situated in the well-known "WYE VALLEY" DISTRICT, all parts of which are within easy reach, including: Tintern Abbey, Raglan Castle, Symonds Yat, The Buckstone, The Speech House, etc.

Proprietress,
very comfort.

EXCELLENT CUISINE AND CELLAR. CHARGES MODERATE.

For Tariffs, etc., apply MISS L. MORGAN.

The Angel Hotel as advertised in 1905

87

From at least 1822 the Williams family kept the **Angel** until the 1850s when William Mills ran the 'Agricultural and Commercial Inn' with 'Mills Coaches, to and from Chepstow daily, along the Valley of the Wye, through Llandogo and Tintern, passing Wyndcliff and Piercefield'. Mills was a notable stage-coachman worthy of an obituary in the *Beacon* of 1879:

The Late Mr. William Mills, – This week another of the race of stage-coachmen now fast disappearing was committed to his last resting place at Monmouth. Mr. William Mills who formerly kept the Black Swan Inn and subsequently the Angel Hotel had a coaching career of about forty years and in his day was a noted man on the road. He was a good and plucky driver and met with very few accidents. His first coach was the *Champion* which ran between Gloucester and Barford and was afterwards named the *Forester*. His next engagement was to drive between Thatcham and Bristol, for Mrs. Philmerty. After several years in that employ he took charge of an opposition coach started by Cooper & Co. over the same ground, and later on of the Bath and Bristol Mail. For two or three years he drove from Bristol to Hereford and then Monmouth was made the limit of his journey. Mr. Mill's coach was then the fastest mail-coach in the kingdom, with the exception of the *Quicksilver* which plied between Devonport and London, the whole journey to Monmouth being performed at the rate of eleven miles an hour. A misunderstanding having arisen between the post officials at Monmouth and Mr. Mills he was out of harness for about a month pending the decision of the dispute. At the end of that time he was re-instated and continued his journeys for about a week, when he gave his employers notice and started the Wye coach which ran to suit the arrival of the Bristol packets at Chepstow. This was his last enterprise on the road. On the death of his wife he relinquished the tenancy of the Angel and subsequently retired to the quietness and rest of Jones' Almshouses.

Externally, the Angel has not changed in the last 50 years

After Mills left the **Angel**, Edwin Brown, Mary Creeper and Miss L. Morgan kept the hotel, offering an ever-changing range of facilities including a 'Ladies Coffee Room', 'Post Horses and Carriages', excellent Cuisine and Cellar' and a 'Dark Room'. Together with the **Beaufort** and **King's Head**, the **Angel** became a Trust House Hotel in the mid-20th century and closed around 1965.

The Malt House in 2005

The **Malt House** is a stylish place to eat; 'fantastically decorated' and offering 'daytime light lunches' and 'superb tapas' since its reopening in 2004. It appears to occupy the building used by G.P. Tippins & Son as a wholesale maltsters and corn merchants in 1895.

In 2005 on the opposite side of the street an empty building was the former **Black Lion**. It has been dramatically changed since James Lewis took over the 'Black Lion Inn occupied by Mrs. Ann Addis with malthouse, brewhouse, stables etc.' in 1860. Mrs. Addis was a gardener and seedsman, presumably carrying on the business of James Addis, who was also a maltster in 1830. The pub was purpose-built around 1860 and sold Redbrook Fine Ales. The Lewis family continued to run the inn until the last quarter of the 19th century, but it has long-since closed.

The Black Lion sold the local Redbrook Ales

The former Black Lion in 2005

Beyond the former **Black Lion**, a narrow lane called Worcester Street leads past the remaining buildings of the Monmouth Brewery.

On the same side of St. Mary's Street was the **Crown**, licensed as the **Crown and Sceptre** in the 1790s when it was used as a meeting place for the Friendly Society of Tradesmen and Others. From the 1820s Nathaniel, then Ann Porter ran the pub until the 1840s when John Roberts took over the licence and shortened its name to the **Crown**. The attractive building continued to trade as a pub until John Davies who was listed as landlord there in 1871. A smaller establishment situated in St. Mary's Street and known as the **Carpenter's Arms**, was kept by James Jones in 1835 and may have continued as Ben Powles beer retailers of 1842. There is also a suggestion that there was a **Harp Inn** in the early 1800s, whilst the yard of the 18th-century **Lamb** was reached from St. Mary's Street.

The one-time Crown in 2005

On the corner of St. Mary's Street and Almshouse Street was the site of Cossens & Rowland, described as 'ale, stout & cider bottlers & wine and spirit merchants' in 1923. Since the 1950s the building has been demolished and the site redeveloped. On the opposite corner was the **Gloucestershire House**, which, although closed as a pub, still retains its West Country plaque. Thomas Reed was the licensee in 1822 and continued there until his death in 1837, when a detailed inventory was made of the rooms and contents. This survives at the

Gwent Record Office and provides a valuable insight into a pub of that period. Part of the three page inventory reads as follows:

Front bedroom – Upper Floor. Four post Beech bedstead, Feather bed, pair blankets, pair sheets, Bed Quilt, Wash hand stand and jug, Chair and glass, Bedside carpet, White window curtain, Five boxes.
Sitting room – 2nd floor. Mahogany dining table, Mahogany card table, Mahogany chest of drawers, Round oak table, Deal table with drawer, Half a dozen chairs, Chimney glass, Five chimney ornaments, Seven round small pictures, Eight larger pictures.

The Gloucestershire House retains its brewery plaque

There were also three further bedrooms, a front Parlour, kitchen, bar, pantry, brewhouse, three cellars and a loft. The stock included 'Beers & Cider: 412 Gallons of Beer, 93 Gallons of Cider' and 'Spirits: 98 Gallons of Gin, 31 Gallons of Brandy, $9^{1}/_{2}$ Gallons of British brandy, 93 Gallons of Rum, $6^{1}/_{2}$ Gallons of Peppermint'.

John Powell kept the **Gloucestershire House** during the 1840s and '50s, but the pub is not recorded in the 1860s. This could account for the unnamed Public House owned by James Hall, who was made bankrupt at that date leaving an inventory of the 'Household Furniture, Fixtures, Fittings and Effects of Bar and Smoke Room. Beer and other Effects at Public House Monmouth' which is now at the Gloucestershire Record Office. The 1860 inventory certainly describes a similar property with three floors and cellars, a front room well furnished with 24 volumes of the *Encyclopaedia Britannia* plus a cellar full of stock. In 1871 William Dugmore was at the **Gloucestershire House Inn** as a 'brewer, maltster and hop merchant'. The pub remained open under the supervision of Mrs. Daw in 1895 and Reece Jones in the 1920s and '30s before the Stroud Brewery acquired the premises. In 1962 they sold 'All that messuage or Inn in St. Mary's Street and partly in St. James's Street known as the Gloucestershire House Inn with the outbuildings and land' to West Country Breweries who were later taken over by Whitbreads.

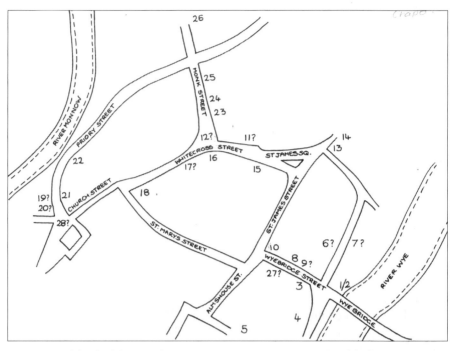

1.	Bridge/Bridge End	19.	Crown & Thistle
2.	Wyebridge Hotel	20.	Horse Shoes
3.	Waterman's Arms	21.	Market Tavern
4.	Ship & Castle/Ship	22.	Swan & Falcon/White Swan
5.	Brockweir Boat	23.	Rose & Crown
6.	Brockweir Boat & Anchor	24.	Herefordshire House
7.	Bear	25.	Ivy Bank/Royal George
8.	Brewer's Arms	26.	Harp
9.	White Hart	27.	Duke of York/Cooper's
10.	**Queen's Head**	Arms	
11.	Whitecross/New Inn?	28.	Lord Nelson
12.	Blue Inn?		
13.	**Old Nag's Head**	Unknown sites:	
14.	Seven Stars		Unicorn?
15.	Labour in Vain/Black Boy		Pear Tree?
16.	Portcullis		Hit or Miss Lucks All?
17.	Black Lion		
18.	**Griffin**	**Bold** open in 2007	

MONMOUTH – Chapter 6: Wye Bridge, St. James Square
& Priory Street

CHAPTER SIX

Monmouth:
WYEBRIDGE, ST. JAMES'S SQUARE & PRIORY STREET

'Wye Bridge, once known as Monmouth Bridge, links South Wales with the Forest of Dean and Gloucester. It was originally a timber structure rebuilt in the 13th and 17th centuries, then widened in 1879. In the past, the banks of the Wye were lined with warehouses, quays and ship-building yards. Heavily loaded barges transported a variety of goods from coal to cider and wine to wheat on the river. Percy Harris described the scene in *An Industrial History of Monmouth:*

> The appearance of the Wyeside at Monmouth like that at Brockweir must have been enchanting. The tall narrow houses at Monmouth, on the waterfront, rising directly from the strand at the river side below the Wyebridge, the trows moored before them as well as on the opposite bank of the Wye. The many wharves above and below the Bridge and the warehouses backed by the higher, Gothic roofs of the town and in the middle distance, the tower and spire of St. Mary's Church make a memorable sight.

In the 1830s Wyebridge and Weirhead Streets were the sites of blacksmiths, coopers, corn factors, bark merchants, maltsters, timber merchants and a lime burner, all served by pubs and beer houses with names reflecting the bridge, the river and its associated industries. Due to the construction of the A40 dual-carriageway in 1960, the majority of the buildings in these streets and along the riverside were demolished, leaving little evidence of the existence of these trades, industries and pubs except in documentary records. From around the 1870s, with the spread of the railway network in the Wye Valley, there was a decline in navigation on the Wye, leaving only ten barges and trows left on the river at Monmouth in 1891.

On the Monmouth side of the Wye Bridge there was a pub called, not surprisingly, the **Bridge Inn**, which dated from the 18th century. In 1835

93

The wharves above Wye Bridge about 1840

List of Licensed Houses

List of Licensed Houses in Wye Bridge ward
Sept 7 1831

Name of Occupiers	Name of Signs
Thomas Perrin	Griffin
William Williams	Angel
Ann Porter	Crown & sceptre
James Jones	Carpenters Arms
Thomas Reed	Glostershire House
Mary Morgan	Queens Head
James Shellard	Brockware Boat
Sam.l Richards	Ship & Castle
Dan.l Collins	Bridge Inn
Thomas Young	White Hart
William Miles	Nags Head
Susanah Morgan	Seven Stars
Ann Warr	New Inn
John Powell	Labour in Vain
Amelia Robinson	
William Price	Herefordshire House
William Sherriff	Royal Oak
Charles Morgan Wm Morgan	Constables of Wye Bridge ward

The inns of Wyebridge ward in 1831

Daniel Collins was the landlord followed by Ann Borfell in the early 1850s. She left the **Bridge** to run another establishment, but returned in 1852 to collect some rent from a new landlord. Unfortunately, her re-appearance must have been far from welcome as she was attacked and beaten by the landlord and seven others in the pub. After being summoned for this assault, the landlord was replaced by Edward Jane, a boat owner, who renamed the pub as the **Bridge End** during his long occupancy. It was in 1884 that Thomas Kirby took over and the inn then became somewhat up-market as the **Wyebridge Hotel**. This did not last, and in 1895 under James Pembridge it became simply the **Wyebridge Inn** and continued to trade as such for another half century.

On the opposite side of Wyebridge Street was the site of a beerhouse kept by Richard Fuller in the 1850s. It later blossomed as the **Watermans Arms**, run

The Watermans Arms was next to the bridge in 1898

by this boat-owning family until it was demolished in 1895 to make way for Monmouth School gates. In its heyday the **Watermans Arms**, overlooking the river and the Wye Bridge, was a three-storied building where the Fuller family were well known as boatmen and had a reputation for rescuing people from drowning in the Wye.

Another boatman's pub was the **Ship and Castle**, which once stood at the bottom of Weirhead Street. In Ann Franks' will of 1760 several messuages, shops and outhouses were listed (including malthouses, brew houses, and timber yards in Wyebridge Street) and a 'Messuage, garden and outhouses known by the sign of the Ship now in possession of James Hodges as tenant'. In 1822 the **Ship** was licensed to Samuel Richards as the **Ship and Castle**. In 1840, when James Hinder was the publican a fire broke out, started by a candle left lying near a straw hamper full of bottled Perry. Luckily, when the straw began to burn, the bottles burst open and the Perry put out the fire! Not long after this incident the inn closed, but the lane leading to it continued to be known as Old Ship and Castle Lane.

On the south side of Weirhead Street was the **Brockweir Boat**, catering for the many thirsty bargemen during the 18th and 19th centuries. In 1820 it was the meeting place of the Loyal Waterloo Lodge of Oddfellows Friendly Society, and was known as the **Old Brockweir Boat** in 1822 when Thomas Lloyd was the publican. Despite a fire in 1870 and a decline in the river trade the **Brockweir Boat** just survived into the 20th century.

This inn should not be confused with the **Brockweir Boat and Anchor**, licensed to John Wood in 1822 for a short period. A licensed property in Granville Street described as 'a big old house' once housed the **Bear** at an unknown period before it was demolished.

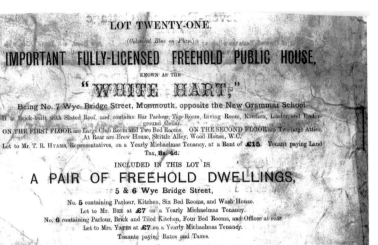

LOT TWENTY-ONE.

(Coloured Blue on Plan.)

IMPORTANT FULLY-LICENSED FREEHOLD PUBLIC HOUSE,

KNOWN AS THE

"WHITE HART,"

Being No. 7 Wye Bridge Street, Monmouth, opposite the New Grammar School.

It is Brick-built with Slated Roof, and contains Bar Parlour, Tap Room, Living Room, Kitchen, Larder, and Under-ground Cellar.
ON THE FIRST FLOOR are Large Club Room and Two Bed Rooms. ON THE SECOND FLOOR are Two large Attics.
At Rear are Brew House, Skittle Alley, Wood House, W.C.
Let to Mr. T. R. HYAMS, Representatives, on a Yearly Michaelmas Tenancy, at a Rent of **£15**. Tenant paying Land Tax, **8s. 4d.**

INCLUDED IN THIS LOT IS

A PAIR OF FREEHOLD DWELLINGS,

5 & 6 Wye Bridge Street,

No. 5 containing Parlour, Kitchen, Six Bed Rooms, and Wash House.
Let to Mr. BEE at **£7** on a Yearly Michaelmas Tenancy.
No. 6 containing Parlour, Brick and Tiled Kitchen, Four Bed Rooms, and Offices at rear.
Let to Mrs. YATES at **£7** on a Yearly Michaelmas Tenancy.
Tenants paying Rates and Taxes.

TOGETHER WITH THE

Right of Cart Way under No. 5,

And the Coach House and Large Garden at Rear of the whole of the foregoing property, with a Right of Way from Wye Bridge Street, is Let to Mr. E. M. TUMMEY, on a Yearly Michaelmas Tenancy, at a Rent of **£5**.

The whole forms

A VERY COMPACT AND DESIRABLE PROPERTY,

Covering an area of about

Sale of the White Hart in 1899

A watercolour of the Queen's Head in about 1888

Two more pubs once existed in Wyebridge Street – the **Brewer's Arms**, kept by Thomas Lugg in 1830, and the 18th-century **White Hart**, which was run during the 19th century by various landlords including James Monnington, another boatman. In 1804 Charles Heath recalled:

> A curious custom prevails at all the ports on the river Severn, but only at Monmouth on the Wye, between the owners and the watermen. Every man, when hired for a voyage, receives a pint of ale as earnest for his services, which is called MUGGING, and if he does not fulfil the labour stipulated for, he is liable to three months imprisonment. Also if the master refuses afterwards to employ the bargeman, the servant has power to demand the wages from him, as tho' he had performed the voyage.

At the corner of Wyebridge Street facing St. James's Street is the **Queen's Head**, an attractive timber-framed building dating from the 16th century. The old inn is surrounded by legends associated with secret hiding places, the Civil War and Oliver Cromwell. An attempt was made to kill him when he was staying at the inn – the would-be assassin leaving bullet-pocked beams as proof of his daring deed. Since then a ghostly figure haunts the inn. During the less disruptive years of the 19th century, the Morgan family kept the **Queen's Head** for a number of years, although in 1831 an incident occurred as recorded by Davies and Kissack:

> In that year trouble was caused by a detachment of the 11th Foot which came to Monmouth after dealing with the enclosure riots in the Forest. They were here for only a short time but when they departed for Chepstow they were followed, according to the *Merlin*, by three enamoured maidens ... and the landlady of the Queen's Head.

A rear view of the Queen's Head

The Queen's Head in 2005

The local newspaper also reported that the inn was in need of restoring in 1884, but it was not carried out until 1922. However, in recent years the inn has been refurbished and remains one of the few pubs still open in Monmouth. Heath, writing in 1804, notes that 'Mr. Powles's house was formerly an Inn, called the Queen's Head, kept by Betty Middleton, afterwards by Mrs. Pugh' – that may have referred to another **Queen's Head**.

A New Inn token of about 1870

There is a slight confusion over the street names of St. James's dating from 1835, and the earlier Whitecross, so it is difficult to locate the site of the **New Inn** which at different periods was listed in St.James's or Whitecross Street. The **New Inn** probably replaced the earlier **Whitecross** kept by William Preece in 1792. The name may have derived from a white cross erected to commemorate those who survived after an outbreak of the plague. This cross may have stood in St. James's Square where the War Memorial now stands. It was probably during the tenancy of William Jones that **New Inn** tokens were struck. Jones was also listed as a plumber, painter and glazier and continued at the inn until the 1890s when Richard Green appears as the last publican before it became 'redundant' in

1906. Also at an unknown site in St. James's Street was the **Blue Inn** recorded as 'ye Blew Inn alehouse' in 1729.

The original main route to London through Ross led from the Eastern or Dixton Gate. According to Charles Heath in 1804:

> The public can never be sufficiently grateful to the characters under whose directions the road was formed between Monmouth and Ross, – since it is allowed by travellers, that, in point of pleasantness and picturesque scenery, it vies with any ten miles within the whole range of the kingdom. Tho' this with the other turnpike roads, were completed at the same period, it was not until about the year 1780 that it became the rival to the road thro' the Forest of Dean. From the nature of the ground, it was always the best road leading from Monmouth for the space of two miles; but Ganarew hill, with many other parts, were in a dreadful state, being full of large rocks and loose stones, that rendered it dangerous both to horse and foot passengers. Such alterations, have since taken place, and are daily going forward, that it is now become the direct post road from London to all parts of South Wales and the South of Ireland.

Nearly 200 years later the present author wrote in *The Old Roads of South Herefordshire*:

> Ross, Hereford and Monmouth Trusts were all responsible for turnpiking various lengths of the route. The piece leading from the said town of Ross by Glewston's Tenders, to the Old Forge was first turnpiked in 1749, followed by the Road leading from Monnow Bridge aforesaid, to the further end of the Parish of Gan y rew in 1755, which left a section between Old Forge and Ganarew, finally taken over by the Hereford Trust in 1819.

Close to Dixon Gate, two pubs competed for business from the passing traffic on this old road to Ross, now simply called Old Dixton Road. The **Old Nag's Head** still exists but the **Seven Stars** closed at the beginning of the 20th century. From 1822 William Miles was kept busy at the **Old Nag's Head** until the 1840s when he was followed by the Williams family. Mrs. Mary Jane kept the inn in 1884, and from thereon there was a succession of landlords. It was eventually acquired by the Alton Court Brewery and was sold to West Country Breweries in 1962. A decade later the **Old Nag's Head** had become a free house and was described as offering 'Real Ale and Beer Garden, [and] Built on the side of Old Dixton Gate'.

The Old Nag's Head in 2005

Heath adds the following information on the four gates of the town:

Of these the Monnow gate might be said to be only remaining; for the east, or Dixton gate, presents solely its circular buttresses that supported its once lofty arch. About 30 years ago, this building was in good preservation, and its summit to be ascended by a regular flight of steps, but it has since been taken down. The left side, as we approach from Ross, has been converted into a dwelling, and now forms the Nag's Head public house. Close under the base of each pillar is a SPRING, whose waters are of the purest quality, and used by the best families for the most comfortable domestic purposes. The Monk and Wye bridge gates were taken down prior to the remembrance of any of the present inhabitants.

Adjoining the **Old Nag's Head** was the **Seven Stars**, licensed to Sarah Hale in 1822. A long line of publicans followed her at the inn which became a Lloyd & Yorath house before closing in 1908.

In Whitecross Street is a long building re-named St. James' Mews which faces Monmouth Library. In 1756 this was the **Labour in Vain** inn 'with the malthouse, stables and other buildings'. The name was originally

100

meant to imply that any attempts to brew ale as excellent as that available there would be a 'labour in vain'. However, it doubtless included the traditional sign of the period representing a house-wife scrubbing a little black boy in a wooden tub. An inn with the same name and sign in Yarnfield in Staffordshire had the following verse underneath:

St James' Mews was once the Labour in Vain

Washing here can now be seen
She scrubs both left and right
Although she'll get him middling clean
She'll never get him white.

The inn was later converted into two separate dwellings, one of which must have continued for a while as the **Labour in Vain** which was kept by James Powell in 1822. This was the inn where the judges lodged during the assizes, and was also a favoured place for the Militia officers' mess. It is assumed that the **Black Boy** of 1709 was the colloquial name for the **Labour in Vain**.

Overlooking the churchyard is Whitecross House – the site of a former inn known by the sign of the **Portcullis** in 1755 and kept at one time by William Marratt. Heath recorded that in his day the house was owned by James Powell, a liquor merchant, and added that:

The one time Portcullis in 2005

101

Our ancestors had either a great deal of leisure time, a great deal of money, or possessed an uncommon thirsty habit, since almost every other house was destined for the retailing of liquor. The Portcullis was a famous Monmouth inn, where entertaining was done on a grand scale. In 1772 the Monmouth Corporation paid the Portcullis £8 10s. 9d. for wining and dining fourteen men. The extensive menu included wine, ale and cider, ham, chicken, duck, lamb, beef, tongue, salmon, lobster and jam tarts, jellies and custards.

Somewhere near Whitecross House is the site of another 18th-century inn called the **Black Lion**, where Dixton parish held their vestry meetings in 1719.

On the corner of Whitecross Street and St. Mary's Street opposite St. Mary's church is the existing **Griffin**, dating from the 18th century and kept at one time by Eleanor Jones who was known 'for the sale of good ale'. It was known as the **Old Griffin** before being rebuilt in the 1830s. At the turn

The Griffin in 2005

of the 19th century it was occupied by Charles Ballinger, who also manufactured mineral water at Glendower Street, enabling him to cater for the more temperate drinkers as well as the imbibers of alcohol. In 2003 the **Griffin** was 'stocked with cocktails and wines, and livelier than most of the pubs in town, with the occasional pub singer and louder music'.

From the **Griffin** a path leads through the churchyard to Priory Street, named after the 12th-century priory church built by Benedictine monks. Its striking oriel window was erected over the entrance around 1490, and is erroneously known as Geoffrey's window after Geoffrey of Monmouth who wrote *History of the Kings of Britain*, some 300 years earlier. Archdeacon Coxe writing in 1801 explains:

> Tradition still points out a small apartment of the priory as the library of Geoffrey of Monmouth; it bears in the ceiling and windows remains of former magnificence, but is much more modern than the age of Geoffrey.

Since the Dissolution, the Priory has been used for a variety of purposes, and may be viewed at certain times. In *A Walk Around Monmouth*, Keith Kissack explains that:

> Priory Street was built in 1837 as a bypass to get the coaches out of Church Street. It remains easily the best addition to the street plan of Monmouth which had become established by the 14th century. It passed along the sloping banks of the Monnow, so it required a viaduct under which were built slaughterhouses. At the same time G.V. Maddox, the local architect of the scheme, built a new Produce Market, now the Monmouth Museum, and gave the other side of the street a fine classical façade.

To enable this redevelopment to take place a number of houses and inns in the Bull Ring were demolished to accommodate the new street, which remains as a fine example of 19th-century improvements.

The **Crown and Thistle** in the Bull Ring was established as an inn around 1800 after being occupied by an apothecary. It was licensed to John Thomas in 1822, but when Charles Edwards ran the inn in 1835 it was purchased by the corporation 'for the purpose of forming a new Market Place'. They paid £2,000 for 'The messuage fronting the Bull Ring in the Market Place with garden, stables and outbuildings called the Crown and Thistle. Now in occupation of Mr. Charles Edwards'. At the same date another inn, which had stood behind the **Crown and Thistle**, and was known as the **Horse Shoe**, was also demolished.

These two inns were shortly replaced by the **Market Tavern**, which sprang up in Priory Street on the corner of Agincourt Square. Susannah Wood, listed in 1842, appears to have been the first innkeeper, and she was followed by members of the Thomas and Price families until the beginning

ALL THAT messuage dwellinghouse or Inn with outbuildings yard and appurtenances thereto adjoining and belonging situate and being Number 26 Agincourt Square in the Town of Monmouth and called the "Market Tavern" now in the occupation of Mrs. Nellie Louisa Meighan and are bounded by the premises next hereinafter described and a messuage and premises now or formerly in the occupation of Josiah Evans and a messuage and premises now or formerly in the occupation of William Hughes and the road or street called Agincourt Square on all or most parts or sides thereof AND ALSO ALL THAT messuage shop and premises situate adjoining the premises above described and being Number 25 Agincourt Square Monmouth aforesaid.

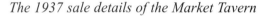

The 1937 sale details of the Market Tavern

*The former Market Tavern, on the corner of Priory Street and Agincourt
Square, re-used by an estate agent in 2005*

of the 20th century. Mrs. Nellie Meighen ran the **Market Tavern** for several decades during which it was acquired by Wintle's Forest Brewery. In 1937 the **Market Tavern** was taken over by the Cheltenham Original Brewery and in the late 1970s the inn finally closed.

When Priory Street replaced Church Street as the main thoroughfare, the **White Swan** in Church Street was rebuilt with a grand entrance and courtyard to face the new street. At Gwent Record Office a bundle of deeds dating from 1709 to 1815 records the history of this inn formerly known as the **Swan and Falcon**. Frank Stephens, the elder, was the innkeeper in 1718 followed by Frank Stephens, the younger, in 1727; then Phillip Fisher took over until 1774 when it was renamed the **White Swan**. In 1822 the inn was licensed to John Lambert and during the 1830s Ann Howe was the landlady before it was rebuilt.

The **White Swan** was reopened in 1839 by the landlord who announced;

'The above newly-built inn is now complete. In its erection and fitting up every provision has been made for the comfort and convenience of those friends who will honour him with their patronage.' The **White Swan** flourished as a coaching inn under John Williams who advertised his 'Commercial Inn and Posting House Opposite the New Market [for] Visitors and Tourists who will find Excellent Accommodation'. It was probably at this period that the **White Swan** was known for its special brew called Early Pearl – a hot drink made with half a pint of boiled ale,

White Swan advertisements:
Top: 1855, Middle:1862, Bottom: 1884

The conveyance of the White Swan in 1886

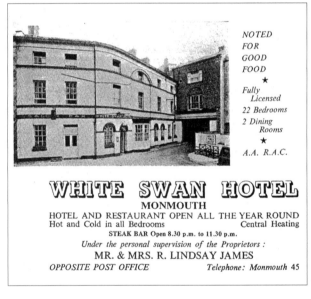

NOTED
FOR
GOOD
FOOD

★

Fully
Licensed
22 Bedrooms
2 Dining
Rooms

★

A.A. R.A.C.

WHITE SWAN HOTEL
MONMOUTH
HOTEL AND RESTAURANT OPEN ALL THE YEAR ROUND
Hot and Cold in all Bedrooms   Central Heating
STEAK BAR Open 8.30 p.m. to 11.30 p.m.
Under the personal supervision of the Proprietors :
MR. & MRS. R. LINDSAY JAMES
OPPOSITE POST OFFICE   Telephone: Monmouth 45

A 1950s advertisement for the White Swan

two pennyworth of gin, a little sugar and a pinch of ginger – which was enjoyed by those waiting for the *Times* or *North Mail* coach to arrive.

John Thomas took over the **White Swan** in the 1860s offering 'Omnibuses to and from each Train, Royal Mail and Coaches to and from Ross' together with 'Posting in all Branches, Hearse and Mourning Coaches'. Thomas was followed by C.J. Knight, who expanded the business into providing 'Wines and Spirits of the Best Quality Only, Private Broughams, Waggonettes and other Carriages, Cobs and Ponies let without drivers when so desired, Saddle Horses and Ponies'. With his stable yard full he also had room to be the 'Head Quarters of the Bicycle Tourist Club'.

In 1886 Mr George Cossens, an ale and porter merchant, purchased:

All that messuage or dwellinghouse and Inn with the Coach House stables brewhouse outbuildings and premises called or known by the name of the White Swan Hotel. Together with the adjoining yard or passage known as the White Swan Passage all situate lying and being between Church Street and Priory Street.

Cossens still owned the **White Swan** in 1911 when it became redundant, but it was later relicensed to Charles Curtis during the 1920s and '30s. After World War Two, Mr. & Mrs. Lindsay James were supervising the 22-bedroomed hotel which was noted for good food and had a steak bar in the late 1950s. It was then kept by Geoffrey Payne followed by David Lawton and John Jacobs, who were able to cater for 'Conference and functions facilities for 150 people'. Trade must have fallen off and only the White Swan Yard remains as a reminder of this old inn.

The yard of what was once the White Swan Hotel

Linking Priory Street with Whitecross Street is Monk Street, named after the monks who built the priory. Although Monk Street dates from the 14th century, only one early inn is known in the area by the author – this was the **Rose and Crown** of 1702 situated in a minor street called St. Nicholas on the east side of Monk Street. Nearby, in the 19th century was the **Herefordshire House**, which was somewhere between the Working Men's Club (now the Art Centre) and Monks Gate. John Price kept the **Herefordshire House** in 1822, and from 1830 William Price was the tenant until it closed around 1871. He remained there despite the sale in 1851 of 'the messuage used as a Public House and called the Herefordshire House near Monks gate' for a sum of £890. The pub was the meeting place of the Herefordshire House Friendly Society formed in 1821, and one of their statements dated 1841 makes interesting reading.

STATEMENT OF THE FUNDS
OF THE
Herefordshire House Friendly Society,
MONMOUTH.
From May 28th, 1840, to May 25th, 1841.

RECEIPTS.	£	s.	d.	DISBURSEMENTS.	£	s.	d.
Contributions of Members	240	9	6	Paid on Interest	95	0	0
Funerals	72	18	0	—— Twenty-two Members being ten years with- out relief	77	0	0
Interest of Money	87	6	0	—— Funerals	74	17	0
Pall	0	11	0	—— Sick Members	121	14	11
Dinner for 1840	25	17	6	—— Committee	0	10	0
Entrance	2	7	6	—— Dinner and extra for 1840	28	17	6
Fines on Feast Day	2	12	6	—— Colourmen	0	3	4
—— for third night	1	11	0	—— Cheeks	20	4	8
——— not serving Stewards	1	17	6	—— Clerk's Salary	6	6	0
Proposition of Men	0	7	0	—— Dispensary and filling up	6	16	0
Money in the Committee Meeting, May 28th, 1840	62	1	4½	—— Inspecting Property and noticing Money	2	4	0
				—— Law charges	0	12	0
	497	18	10½	—— Visiting sick	0	19	3
Disbursements	440	19	4	—— Stewards putting money out	0	3	4
				—— Paper and Books	0	5	0
In the Box	56	19	6¼	—— William Price for received Interest	1	0	0
Principal at Interest on Mortgage	1823	0	0	—— Printing Statements and Notices	1	2	0
				—— Drawing up Statement	0	3	6
Total Stock	£1879	19	6½	—— Back to Benjamin Wood	0	18	10
				—— Drawing up returns to Parliament	2	2	0
					440	19	4
				Cash in the Box	56	19	6¼
					£497	18	10½

THOMAS WALTERS, Clerk.

The 1840-41 accounts of the Herefordshire House Friendly Society

On the east side of Monk Street is a large Georgian house, now apartments, which was originally called Ivy Bank and run as a lodging house from 1931 by Ethel Jones, whose late husband had purchased the property in 1918. After her death in 1952 it became the **Ivy Bank**, a fully licensed hotel owned by John Watts Hotels Ltd. When it was sold in 1954 it included 14 bedrooms, 3 bathrooms, 2 lounges, a lounge bar including a 'mahogany counter having attractive arched ornamentation with Corinthian pillars. The counter is served by a two-pull beer engine'. There was also a cellar

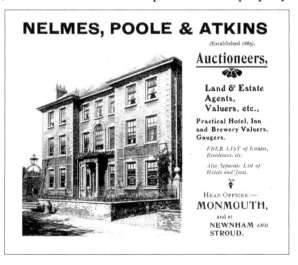

Ivy Bank for sale in the 1900s

Ivy House was a lodging house in the 1930s

that was 'reached by an easy staircase from the ground floor, and contains compartments of beers, wines and spirits'. After this sale it was renamed the **Royal George** with a 'Licensed Bar and Restaurant', but did not survive as an hotel for any length of time and is now residential apartments.

Also in Monk Street, lying north of Priory Street, was the **Harp** of 1801, which was one of two small tenements, which were converted into Parade House by a local banker in the mid-19th century. He Gothicised the windows and added a fine staircase.

With so many pubs, inns, taverns and hotels,

The Ivy Bank became the Royal George in the 1950s but was unsuccesful as a hotel and is now private residential apartments

MONMOUTH.

The LORD NELSON INN, & Five Freehold Messuages.

TO BE SOLD BY AUCTION,
By *JAMES WOAKES*,

At the LORD NELSON INN, Monmouth, on Saturday, the Second day of December, 1815, between the hours of Four and Six in the Afternoon, subject to Conditions of Sale which will be then produced,

ALL that substantial modern-built and well-accustomed INN, called and known by the name of THE LORD NELSON, with the Yard, Stabling, and Appurtenances thereto belonging, now in the Occupation of Mr. Richard Miles.

Also, all those Five newly-erected MESSUAGES or TENEMENTS, with the Yards and Appurtenances thereunto belonging, and which are now or lately were, in the respective Occupations of William Williams, William Taylor, Richard Baker, James Browne, and —— Caple.

The above Inn consists of good under-ground Cellaring, a good large Kitchen, Parlour, Sashed Bar, a spacious Dining Room, and every other Convenience suitable for an Inn, and is eligibly situated for business, in the High-Town, near to the Market Place in Monmouth, and the Five Messuages, which are also situated in the Town of Monmouth, will be Sold in such Lots as shall be fixed upon at the Time of Sale.

The respective Tenants will show the Premises, and for further Particulars apply to Mr. Built, Solicitor, or the Auctioneer, Hereford.

Sale of the 'modern built' Lord Nelson in 1815

it was not surprising that a temperance movement was established in Monmouth as early as 1839. After a shaky start it did not attract a great following until later in the century. The vicar formed a company to finance a British Workman Public House in 1877, but the attempt to wean men from beer to tea and coffee did not succeed. There was the Castle Temperance Hotel in Priory Street at the turn of the 19th century, which catered for visitors, tourists and cyclists; and for the locals the Sons of the Temperance Benefit Society held meetings at the Working Man's Institute in Monk Street from 1910. The movement campaigned for Sunday closing which was adopted in Monmouth during World War One and repealed in 1961.

Before leaving the town of Monmouth, it is worth mentioning a number of named pubs that once existed in the town. There was the **Unicorn** of 1734, the **Pear Tree** of 1876. and the **Hit or Miss Luck's All**, which was licensed to Thomas Harrison in 1822 but did not succeed as a pub or beer house. The **Cooper's Arms** of 1796, formerly the **Duke of York**, was in Wyebridge Street and was still funcrioning in 1850. There was also the **Lord Nelson**, which must have opened after Nelson's visit in 1802 but ceased to exist after an auction sale in 1815. It was situated in 'the High Town next to the Market Place' in 1815.

110

CHAPTER SEVEN

Dixton, Mayhill, Wyesham & Redbrook

The parish of Dixton lies one mile north-east of Monmouth and extends on both sides of the Wye to include Hadnock, Mayhill, Wyesham and part of Redbrook. Before the A40 dual-carriageway was constructed in 1960 the Norman church of St. Peter's at Dixton stood quietly by the river Wye, but due to its position it is susceptible to severe flooding as described by Charles Heath in 1828:

> The Church, from standing so near to the shore, is frequently visited by the Floods of the Wye, – whose waters sometimes force themselves through the windows and doors, – leaving the interior not only a wreck, but rendering it necessary to suspend the performance of Public Worship. – In 1795 and 1798, the waters covered the hedges, on each side of the turnpike road.

This road, which led to Ross, was made by the turnpike trustees and after many improvements it became the 'direct post road from London to all parts of South Wales and the South of Ireland'.

In 1862 there were a number of 'clergy and gentry' living in Dixton parish, whilst those involved in the trades and industries lived mainly in the Redbrook area. At that time the trades included ironfounding, brewing, malting, farming, chemical working, beer retailing and innkeeping. Out of the 25 named and licensed premises open at varying dates, only three remained to offer food and drink in 2005. These are the **Royal Oak**, on the Hereford Road, the **May Hill Hotel** at May Hill and the **Bell** at Redbrook.

From Monmouth the Hereford Road, a continuation of Monk Street, leads north from the former toll house. This road was turnpiked by the Monmouth Turnpike Trust in 1755 and is now the A466 leading past the remains of the County Gaol – the gatehouse re-used by Monmouth Girls School. The Gaol was built in 1790 and, before closing in 1869, several executions took place there. This gave name to Hangman's Hill, lying opposite the gaol, where it is said the **Hangman's Inn** once stood, although no documentary evidence has been found. Life in the gaol was extremely harsh, but if a prisoner could pay then certain privileges were available. In 1820 the adjutant of the Militia was charged and eventually gaoled for assault, but by paying the appropriate backhanders he was allowed to use the magistrate's room, stay up till 10 pm, see friends and drink wines, spirits and beers.

AN OLD ESTABLISHED FREEHOLD FULLY-LICENSED INN,

KNOWN AS THE

"ROYAL OAK."

Situate on the East Side of Old Hereford Road, within One Mile of Monmouth, well set back from Main Road, and entered by Glazed Porch with Tiled Floor, and contains Tap Room, Bar, Bar Parlour, match-boarded in two colours, Private Parlour, Back Lobby, Kitchen, Wash House and Pantry. Underground Cellars. Above are Sitting Room and Three Bed Rooms. All Newly Decorated and in Good Order.

Adjoining are Slated Barn, Stone and Tiled Stable for Four Horses, Large Fowl House, Two Piggeries, and Two Vegetable Gardens with Large and Sheltered Orchard.

ALSO

LAWN AND PLEASURE GROUNDS LAID OUT FOR TEAS AND ENTERTAINMENTS.

The whole lies compactly together, adjoins property belonging to Colonel Lloyd, and contains

5 Acres, 1 Rood, 18 Perches.

Sale of the Royal Oak in 1899

A mile further up the Hereford Road is the **Royal Oak**, dating from the 18th century, where in 1835 William Fuller – a police constable – 'fought and arrested two horse thieves'. Without assistance he took both men and horses to the police station and the following year was promoted to sergeant. The Bird family ran the **Royal Oak** in the mid-19th century followed by a succession of landlords who successfully kept the pub open. In the 1970s the **Royal Oak** was one of several inns that were described as being 'The Last Pub in Wales'. At that time visitors could get 'A Traditional Sunday Lunch, Home-cooked Bar Meals, Real Ales, Caravan Park, Beer Garden and Childrens' play area ... all in a relaxed and cosy atmosphere'.

Before reaching Buckholt on the Hereford Road there is the junction of Manson Lane, where a low, whitewashed property of two stories and an attic formerly served as the **Manson's Cross Inn** until the mid-1960s. The

The Royal Oak in 2005

building dates from the late 17th century and its date-stone indicates that it was converted into a public house by Philip Endale to cater for those travelling on the Monmouth to Hereford road after it was turnpiked in 1755. Thomas Moxley, the landlord in 1790, was known for his fruit growing skills, and Heath recorded the inn in 1804. However, it was

Once the Manson's Cross Inn

not apparently listed again until 1871 when James Powles kept the hostelry. Various landlords ran the inn until it was acquired by the Ross-based Alton Court Brewery. They eventually sold 'All that messuage or Inn at Monmouth known as the Mansons Cross Inn with the outbuildings yard and land thereto belonging and adjoining containing in the whole 1 acre and 25 perches or thereabouts' to West Country Breweries in 1962. It is now called *Hen Dafarn* – the Welsh for 'Old Inn'.

The Hereford Road ascends to the wooded slopes of Buckholt forming the boundary between Welsh Monmouthshire and English Herefordshire. Just within Monmouthshire on the roadside is the former **Plough**, which was kept

THE FULLY-LICENSED FREEHOLD ROADSIDE INN,

KNOWN AS

"THE PLOUGH,"

SITUATE

At the Buckholt, in the Borough of Monmouth on the East side of the Old Hereford Road, one-and-a-half miles from Monmouth. Comprising

STONE AND TILED HOUSE, containing LARGE KITCHEN, TAP ROOM, PARLOUR.

Below are Cellar, Old Brewhouse, and Offices, and above are 3 Bed Rooms.

Also BRICK and TILED CYDER MILL, HOUSE, and LOFT.

ADJOINING IS A STONE AND TILED THREE-ROOMED COTTAGE,

With Garden, Sub-let to Mrs. WEATHERBY, at £2 10s. a Year

Also GARDEN, PIGGERIES, and STRIP OF GRASS LAND, and ORCHARD fronting Main Road.

The whole comprises part of No. 18 and No. 69 on the Ordnance Plan, and has an area of about

3 Roods,

Let to Mr. GEORGE WATKINS, on a Yearly Michaelmas Tenancy, at a Rent of £5., and Sub-let at £13 5s. to HENRY WOOD. Tenant paying Land Tax 4s. 8d.

The Tithe, if any, belonging to the MARQUIS OF WORCESTER, is included in the Sale.

Sale of the Plough in 1899

The Plough in retirement in 2005

by James Smith in the 1870s and '80s. He was followed by Frederick Taylor, who appears to be the last landlord in 1910.

From Mansons Cross an old road leads past Cannes Farm where a farmer was retailing beer in 1871. A delightful field path runs parallel to the lane through Leasbrook, where the **Curled Cat** stood behind Inglewood and opposite Dixton church in the mid-19th century.

From Dixton church a stretch of the original road leading south towards Monmouth now serves as a useful parking place to explore the riverside, church and the Wye Valley Walk. According to E.T. Davies and Keith Kissack a licence to sell cider and Perry was granted to John Pearce in 1881 at the **Bee Hive**, but the precise site at Dixton is unknown. Another pub known as the **Fleece** in 1812 existed possibly in the Dixton area.

The old road from Dixton led into Monmouth at Dixton Gate, where the **Cock Ale House** would have provided a welcome sight. In 1722 Charles Evans, a forgeman, was the tenant of the 'messuage formerly in the possession of and built by James Ashman'. When Monmouth was recycling its old cinders from the medieval forges for use in other Wye Valley production sites, this inn was referred to as 'the Cock Alehouse and the Iron Cinders Mine' in 1769. This beer house must have stood next to the **Nag's Head**, and may have been an earlier name for the **Seven Stars** (see chapter six).

From Monmouth the Wye Bridge, known as Monmouth Bridge in the 13th century, leads across the river to Hadnock, May Hill, Wyesham and Redbrook – all part of Dixton parish and the only portion of Monmouthshire lying east of the Wye. Heath in 1804 explained that:

> The Gate on this bridge, formed a principal defence to this part of the town, - but it appears to have been taken down many years ago, since I do not meet with any person among the inhabitants capable of affording me information of its existence.

He added that

> The father of H. Barnes, esq. of the Fort, built the house at the extremity of the Bridge, which was for many years a public house, and called The New Inn.

Buildings shown on a plan of 1800 on the east side of Wye Bridge have long since gone including the **New Inn**. During the 19th century the Gas Works, the Brick & Lime Works, the Saw Mills and Mayhill Station were all built on the east bank. The railway station served the Ross to Monmouth line which opened in 1873 and was extended a year later across a viaduct to Monmouth Troy station. The railway was closed down in 1964, but remains of the viaduct stand as a reminder of the railway age.

Beyond the busy junction of the Forest of Dean and Wye Valley roads, a turning on the left follows the Wye upstream to Hadnock, where in 1797 a 'small tenement near the town of Monmouth called the Hurdle House now in the occupation of John Partridge' was known to have been a licensed premises for in 1812 the **Hurdle House** was conveyed to John Stead. The whereabouts of the house is unknown, but a farm of that name existed in 1862.

Between the roads leading to the Forest of Dean and Wyesham is the **May Hill Hotel**, another 'last pub in Wales' – this time on the east bank of the Wye. In the 18th century the property accommodated lodgers before becoming a school, and did not open as 'The May Hill Hotel and Public House' until the beginning of the 20th century. Frank Shelley may have been

A 1930s advertisement for the May Hill Hotel

The May Hill Hotel in 2005

the first proprietor of this establishment, described in 1924 as 'Mayhill Hotel, Family and Commercial, board residence, luncheons, dinners & teas; bath (h. & c.), electric light throughout'. Mrs. E. Braint became the manageress during the 1930s when the hotel was serving Ind Coope and Allsopp Burton Ales to its customers.

There was another pub nearby standing on the corner of the road leading to the Gas Works at May Hill, called the **Traveller's Rest** and run by the Morgan family during the 19th century. In 1842 an incident occurred when

Sale of the Traveller's Rest in 1899

David Howells was arrested by a policeman for being drunk at the inn, but the policeman was also accused of being drunk. The outcome was that Howells was found to be 'drunk' whilst the policeman was 'only not sober'.

There was also the **George** at May Hill, listed from 1860 and run by three different women until the end of the century when it apparently closed.

From May Hill a choice of routes lead up to the scenic view on top of the Kymin, either a footpath – part of the Offa's Dyke Path – offering a steep ascent by foot, or a more leisurely drive by car following a zig-zagging lane which was commissioned as a carriageway in 1799 at a cost of £250 and completed a few years later. The Kymin is well known for its outstanding views, the Round House and the Naval Temple which are in the care of the National Trust. The temple, built in 1801, commemorates British admirals including Lord Nelson who visited the site in 1802. The Round House and Pleasure Ground were constructed in 1794 by a group of Monmouth gentlemen as a place where they could eat, drink and play in pleasant and secluded surroundings. They were members of the Kymin Club and Heath relates how they met

> during the most pleasant part of the Summer season ... for the purpose of dining together, and spending the day in a social and friendly manner. The Dinner, which consists of a cold collation, is provided by each member in his turn, with a dessert of fruits, and wines to a certain limitation.

117

The Kymin in 2005

From the mid-19th century the Kymin became a popular place for all to visit, with an exhibition of flowers, fruit and poultry attended by a 'good band' in 1856. In 1901 the public were invited to attend tennis, croquet and refreshments at the Kymin Tower and Pleasure Grounds by riding ponies and donkeys from Wye Bridge. The Refreshment Rooms on the Kymin were open during the 1920s and '30s, and on several occasions more recently.

At the Kymin a delightful path leads down to a hollow-way, once the old coach road leading from Staunton to Monmouth. On the side of the road near Beaulieu Farm is York Cottage, the site of the **Duke of York Inn** at Broadstone. Apparently it flourished in the 18th century before this road was replaced by the new turnpike road of 1831, but its known documentation dates from the 1870s when W. Jenkins was the licensee,

The one-time Duke of York in 2005

followed by Albert Jones and Samuel Davison before closing as a pub in the early 20th century.

From Wye Bridge the Redbrook Road and the riverside path, which now forms a section of the Wye Valley Walk, both pass the site of the **Three**

Salmons Inn at Halfway House. This inn was established by the mid-18th century and was occupied by Mrs. Miles in 1807, William Hughes in 1822 and William Preece in 1862, after which the pub closed.

Redbrook in 1862 was described in a Monmouthshire directory as:

> a village, two miles S. by E. from Monmouth, partly in the parish of Dixton, in this county, and partly in the parish of Newland, county of Gloucestershire; pleasantly situated on the banks of the Wye, on the road to Gloucester. The two counties are here separated by a small brook that runs past the village. An iron foundry and brewery belonging to Messrs. Thomas Burgham and Son, together with some flour mills, and maltings are the principal branches of trade now carried on here.

There was also a hop merchant, blacksmith, saw miller, tinplate workers and six inns open including the already mentioned **Three Salmons**.

When Mr. and Mrs. Hall were touring the Wye Valley in 1861 they left Monmouth where 'The tourist has a good choice of inns – a matter of no small importance', and approaching Redbrook

> we reach a very different scene ... for rising above a thick foliage, is the dense column of smoke that tells the whereabouts of a manufactory ... There are quays here; we note the bustle of commerce, – other life than that of the stream and the forest. The masts of many barges rise from the river: they are loading or unloading.

Over the centuries Redbrook became an industrial place where the waters of the Valley and Red brooks powered blast furnaces, copper smelting and tin-plate works, several corn mills, a 17th-century paper mill and three breweries. Not all of these were working at the same time, and most had ceased by the end of the 19th century. Iron ore and charcoal were readily available from the Forest of Dean whilst transportation was supplied by barges on the river Wye. Industrial growth was aided by the construction of the Monmouth Tramway from Coleford via Redbrook to May Hill in 1817, the completion of the Monmouth to Chepstow turnpike road in 1824, and the opening of the Wye Valley Railway in 1876. With the gradual decline in these industrial activities, Redbrook has slowly been transformed into a delightful place.

Although several of the past and present pubs of Redbrook were featured in *The Pubs of the Royal Forest of Dean*, it is appropriate to include some of them here, together with the others in the Monmouthshire parish of Dixton. A Redbrook Brewery was established in 1825 by Richard Sims, and before 1842 the Redbrook Upper Brewery was acquired by James Hall. In 1853 the *Beacon* newspaper displayed a notice from James Hall, thanking everyone for their support. This was two years before he advertised the brewery 'To be Let or Sold ... [with its] Genteel Residence [and] large commodious Malt-house, capable of making 1,200 quarters of Malt per season, with a good trade; also a small compact three-quarter Brewery attached, with a constant supply of excellent water'. The brewery was auctioned two years later at the **Beaufort Arms** in Monmouth. The sale notice included the following:

> The Malthouse is large and convenient, and the Brewery is very compact. The House and Premises are pleasantly situated, abundantly supplied with pure spring water, and offer a desirable opportunity for making a mere investment, or for enabling a purchaser to carry on the extensive Malting and Brewery business long connected with the property.

The Redbrook Brewery, run by Charles Herbert, was acquired by Thomas Burgham in 1856. His family ran and extended the business which supplied at least 22 licensed properties either owned or tied to the Redbrook Brewery. In 1840 three brewers were listed, but by 1849 only Charles Herbert and Jane Hall were brewing.

At its industrial height Redbrook was said to have 'consisted largely of inns' – perhaps an exaggerated figure for the nine known licensed premises that were established at various dates throughout the early to mid-19th century. Opposite the Old Brewery, on the corner of the Wye Valley road and the steeply ascending road to the Forest of Dean, was the **Bush Inn**. James Madley and members of his family ran it from at least 1822, whilst in

Proposed sale of the Redbrook Brewery in 1855

The Old Brewery House in 2003

120

AN EXCELLENTLY SITUATED ROADSIDE INN
(FREEHOLD),

KNOWN AS THE

"BUSH" INN, REDBROOK.

In the Parish of Dixton Hadnock, opposite Redbrook Station on the Chepstow and Monmouth Railway, at the junction
of the Coleford, Chepstow, and Monmouth Roads.

The Entrance is opposite the Station, and gives access to Bar, Lobby, Tap Room, large Living Room, with Private
Entrance Dairy, Kitchen and Cellars. Above are Club Room and Four Bed Rooms.

Adjoining are Stabling for Four Horses, Shed, Slaughter, and Cyder Houses.

At the Rear is a Large Garden lying between the Railway and Garden occupied by Mrs. EVANS. The whole forms
part of No. 481 on Ordnance Plan, and contains about

1 Rood and 14 Perches.

Let to Mr. O. A. BURGHAM, on a Yearly Michaelmas Tenancy, with other property not included in this sale, at a
Rent of **£25** and **£19** is the Rent apportioned on this Lot during the continuance of the Tenancy. Tenant paying
Land Tax, **11s. 10d.** Tithe Free.

Sale of the Bush Inn in 1899

1862 Philip Jones, a butcher, kept the inn over a period of three decades. Despite a series of later landlords the **Bush** survived as a pub into the mid-1990s. It was much used by ramblers following either the Offa's Dyke Path or the Wye Valley Walk, which meet at Redbrook creating some excellent walking routes.

The property called the **Old Inn** at the top of Upper Redbrook was probably the

The one-time Bush Inn in 2003

Queen's Head kept by Richard Underwood in the mid-19th century and the Hawkins family from at least 1895 until 1939. The inn closed around 1959, but the property was advertised for sale at the beginning of the 21st century as:

> a former inn and two attached cottages, originating from the 17th century, now beautifully restored throughout, providing flexible well arranged accommodation in two distinct parts, together with outbuildings and landscaped gardens with terraces, all adjoining a natural trout stream and waterfall running alongside the gardens.

Opposite was the **Founder's Arms**, licensed to William Page in 1831, Ann Page in 1842, and Charles Morgan in 1862, before a succession of different landlords took over this Redbrook Brewery house until it closed in the early 1900s.

At Lower Redbrook there were two pubs in 1848 overlooking the Wye and situated below the former tin-plate works which ceased production in 1961. The **King's Head** emerged from a beer house of 1840, run by Barnabas Lambert in 1859, whilst from at least 1879 to 1906 the Taylors kept the inn. It was later taken over by Arnold, Perrett & Company of Hereford and passed to the Cheltenham Original Brewery in 1937 as 'all that messuage tenement and dwellinghouse or Inn and premises called or known

Two old Redbrook pubs:
Top: The Old Inn; probably the Queen's Head. Bottom: The Founder's Arms

ALL THAT messuage tenement or Inn known as The Bell Inn situate at Lower Redbrook in the Parish of Newland in the County of Gloucester TOGETHER with the garden stable brewhouse and maltroom thereunto belonging and occupied therewith and all other outbuildings and appurtenances thereunto belonging and also the roadway leading to the stable from the highway leading from Redbrook Monmouth to Chepstow TOGETHER with the site thereof and the land occupied therewith.

The 1937 sale of the Bell Inn

by the name of the King's Head Inn with the garden thereto'. Since then it has closed.

The **Bell** is the only surviving pub in Redbrook although it was temporarily closed in 1992 and reopened as the **Fish and Game**, before becoming a bed and breakfast establishment. At the beginning of the 21st century it was reopened with a flourish by a new landlord. The **Bell** had opened by 1862 under the supervision of Joseph Marfield, and throughout the 1880s and '90s James Beard was the licensee. When Frances Hudson was the landlady in 1937 this Arnold, Perrett and Co. house was acquired by the Cheltenham Original Brewery including 'garden, stable, brewhouse and maltroom'. It had become a free house by the late 1980s when the

Formerly the Fish and Game, it became 'Bed and Breakfast' but is now the Bell

The Bell Inn in 2003

THE BELL
Redbrook

Free House

Mine Hosts:
Sue and Maurice Rogers

Tel: Monmouth 3 137

An Old Country Inn
Modernised to a high standard,
offering a comfortable lounge
and beer patio overlooking
the River.
Bar meals always available with
steaks, fish and beautifully
cooked cider baked hams
on the menu.

1990 advertisement for the Bell Inn

'Old Country Inn' was offering 'a comfortable lounge and beer patio overlooking the River. Bar meals always available with steaks, fish and beautifully cooked cider baked hams'.

Three other licensed premises existed at Redbrook in the early part of the 19th century. There was the **White Hall** licensed to William Taylor in 1822 and 1830 before Edward Williams took over from 1835 to 1842. The **Cellars** was licensed to James Hall in 1830 and 1831 – this may have been his first attempt in the beer business before acquiring the Redbrook Brewery. Then there was the **Redbrook Arms** of 1840 to 1842 run by Thomas Howells. The exact whereabouts of these three pubs are not known by the author.

CHAPTER EIGHT

Penallt, Cwmcarvan, Mitchel Troy & Llandogo

The hilly, remote and scenic parish of Penallt lies just south of Monmouth with the river Wye forming its eastern boundary. In the early 19th century Heath wrote:

> This place, which was surrounded by a fine and extensive Common (lately inclosed), is celebrated for the production of the Breccia, or Pudding Stone, formed more or less compact. Very excellent mill-stones are cut in dove-tailed burrs, which millers pronounce equal to the very valuable French stones; and the surrounding counties are also supplied with cider-mills from the quarries of Mr. Wm. Williams, of this parish. ... The communication of this place with the opposite side of the country, is kept open by means of a ferryboat, which conveys over both horse and foot passengers. The parish is supplied with coal from the Forest of Dean.

Today, the hills and river bank of Penallt are best explored by foot following the numerous footpaths and tracks, easily accessed from the east bank of the Wye at Redbrook by crossing the old railway bridge to the only surviving inns – the **Boat** and the **Bush**. In 1871 four inns, two shops and a butcher served a population of around 450 who were mainly employed as stone masons, carpenters, farmers, wood dealers, market gardeners, millers and boot and shoe makers. Others were employed in the paper mills at Whitebrook and in the tin-plate works at Redbrook.

Due to the steepness of the narrow roads leading to Penallt church, a story exists that the mourners who carried a coffin for burial would rest on the way at the 'coffin seat' to catch their breath and refresh themselves with 'jars of home-brewed ale and cider as well as substantial meat pies'. One tale surving from this tradition is about a wealthy but miserly farmer who had died and was being carried by the funeral party, who were well fortified by ale. They stopped at their usual resting place and laid the coffin on the ground with a jolt. A groaning sound was heard, so the coffin lid was opened, and the old farmer sat up asking for a glass of water. When he eventually died his widow demanded there would be no stopping at the coffin seat.

In the past beekeepers produced mead, and several cottages and farms with their own cider-presses and brew-houses were able to make a powerful brew before the beer retailers and licensed premises took over during the 19th century. Mary Stevens and Thomas Hudson were both recorded as beer retailers in Penallt between 1860 and 1880, but in 1884 Thomas from Redbrook erected a 'cider mill and other buildings ... bounded by the Wye

Valley Railway, Land of the Duke of Beaufort and a footway leading from the River Wye to the Lone Lane'.

At the riverside were two ferries, the Upper and the Lower ones, both connecting Penallt to Redbrook. At the Upper Ferry, the **Wheatsheaf** was converted from a water-mill into a beer house

The old Wheatsheaf in 2005

The Wye in flood at the Boat Inn at Penallt in December 1997

The Boat at Penallt from the railway bridge in 2005

which was run by James Jones in 1871. It is an attractive stone building traditionally known as a cider house where cider continued to be made into the 1960s. An unfortunate incident occurred during its later cider making years, when a pony was used to turn the mill stone, but the animal was too large for the cider mill and caused havoc.

The **Boat** lies below the railway bridge that was built in 1876 to carry the Wye Valley Railway over the river. A footbridge was attached in 1955 which, despite the railway being closed in 1964, continues to be used as a right-of-way and forms an important link of the Wye Valley Walk. During the 1870s and '80s the Williams family ran the **Boat**, and at the end of the 19th century the inn was described as a busy place where barges were moored while the bargees enjoyed a drink. The water from the springs at the rear of the pub was apparently piped across the river to be used at the Redbrook Brewery.

In the 1990s the **Boat** was described in the author and her husband's *Paths and Pubs of the Wye Valley*:

Food and refreshment are good and the beer selection includes a host of beers, with funny names like Sneck Lifter, Cocker Hoop, Red Fox, Tanners Jack and Free Miner. Lagers and ciders cater for more ordinary palates and vin ordinaire is available in bottle and glass. A list of hedgerow wines is also offered. The menu contains sufficient variety and we personally appreciate the accent on unusual vegetarian dishes. Perennial favourites like Ploughman's with plenty of good English cheese and homemade soups satisfy most ramblers.

TO BE SOLD BY

AUCTION,

BY MR. MICHAEL DAVIS,

At the Lion Inn, Trelleck,

On Wednesday, the 13th of May 1829,

AT THREE O'CLOCK IN THE AFTERNOON,
UNLESS SOONER DISPOSED OF BY PRIVATE CONTRACT,
ALL THAT WELL-ACCUSTOMED

Public House,

CALLED

THE BUSH,

TOGETHER WITH

STABLING, BARN, SLAUGHTERHOUSE,

ORCHARD, GARDEN,

And a large Room, (26 feet by 12) used for Public Purposes,
THEREUNTO ADJOINING AND BELONGING.

The Bush auctioned at the Lion at Trelleck in 1829

It was also known for Live Folk and Jazz and was featured in the Good Food and Good Beer guides.

The **Bush** at Penallt is situated at least a mile south of the old parish church in the centre of the present village. It can be accessed from Lone Lane leading from the riverside or from a turn off the B4293 road from Monmouth. Overlooking the Wye Valley, the **Bush** was originally a property belonging to the Duke of Beaufort, and apparently its cider-mill had a date stone of 1714. It was auctioned in 1829 together with 'a Newly Erected, and as yet Unfinished, Dwelling House'.in the grounds.

After the death of the landlord, Thomas Gleed, in the early 1890s, the **Bush** was put up for sale again in 1892 as 'The Very convenient and Fully Licensed Public House Being the only one in the village and known as The Bush Inn with Gardens and Land'.

The Bush at Penallt in 2005

Above: The Bush sign

Left: A charming corner of the Bush Inn

After the sale George Gleed took over the licence, and he was followed by several parish families including the Morgans, Matthews, Badhams, Prings, Ricketts and Phillips. In the 1990s Simon and Julie Tupper were at the **Bush** offering 'a fine selection of Traditional Ales and freshly prepared Meals', and in the 21st century the inn is still a friendly, comfortable and relaxing free house with a bar and restaurant and a choice of 'traditional ales, lagers, wines, spirits and soft drinks' and a menu offering 'a fine selection of locally produced fayre'.

In the past Penallt was known for its cider when 'almost every small farm had cider apple trees and cider mills. Cider houses were known to have existed at Church Cottage and Brook Farm, and the **Hoop** of the 1870s and '80s run by the Roberts family was either a beer or cider house. In 1786 Edward Davis wrote:

> No better cider does the world supply
> Than grows along thy borders, gentle Wye;
> Delicious, strong and exquisitely fine,
> With all the friendly properties of wine.

A few years ago there was another pub on the Penallt boundary, but actually in Cwmcarvan parish on the B4293. It was known as the **Gockett**,

129

Above: The Gockett in 2005.   Below: The Gockett signboard from 2000

with evidence to suggest that it was established before 1800. In 1816 Charles Heath briefly mentioned that 'because of its position at the junction of four parishes it was formerly used for meetings of magistrates ... which from its falling into ruins have since been transferred to Trelleck'. According to Bradney 'moor game was fairly plentiful and Charles Heath in 1810 relates that they had recently been destroyed; the last pair that remained having been killed by a notorious poacher who sold the birds at Bristol for a high price. The inn was recently called the Cockett, but by now the Grouse bears testimony to this effect'. In 1825 the property was acquired by Benjamin Green, a victualler from Monmouth, who later sold it to the Morgan family. Various landlords followed, and by the 1990s the **Gockett** had gained a good reputation for food and wine, but for some unknown reason the doors were bolted, the windows boarded up and the signs taken down. In 2007 the former **Gockett** is again in a derelict and neglected state.

Cwmcarvan takes its name from the valley of the Carfan brook, and is a virtually unknown and remote place lying to the west of the B4293. Its church, dedicated to St. Clement, stands in a beautiful position in the midst of a maze of lanes. In 1862 the farming community was served by the **Bush** and the **New Inn**, both at unknown sites. The only other known pub in Cwmcarvan is the **Somerset Arms** on the old road from Monmouth to Raglan. It was open in 1895 when Thomas Prosser was recorded as the innkeeper before it was sold as part of the Duke of Beaufort's estates in 1899. It was purchased by the Alton Court Brewery from Ross, and the beer was either delivered by the brewery or collected from the brewery in Ross until 1962 when the Alton Court Brewery and its pubs were taken over by West Country Breweries and became part of the Whitbread empire. It has now

---

IN THE PARISH OF CWMCARVAN.

THE WELL-KNOWN ROADSIDE INN,

THE

"SOMERSET ARMS,"

(FREEHOLD AND FULLY-LICENSED.)

Being on the Main Monmouth and Raglan Road, Four Miles from the Town of Monmouth, and within 700 yards of Dingestow Station on the Monmouth to Pontypool Branch of the Great Western Railway.

It is well-placed for Trade, is one of the meets of the Monmouthshire Hounds, and is on the borders of the Parish of Cwmcarvan.

Well set back from the Main Road, and contains,

TAP ROOM, BAR-PARLOUR, SITTING ROOM, BACK KITCHEN, CELLAR and FOUR BED ROOMS

Conveniently placed near the House are

STABLE for THREE HORSES, PIG STYES, COAL and OTHER OUT-HOUSES, together with

TWO PRODUCTIVE GARDENS,

The whole being No. 737 on the Ordnance Plan, and contains about

2 Roods and 16 Perches,

Let to Mr. T. W. PROSSER, on a Yearly Michaelmas Tenancy at a Rent of £15 a year. Tenant pays Land Tax, 15s. Tithe 2s. 2d.

NOTE.—This House is being supplied with water by a line of pipes laid from a well in the field at the rear belonging to the Vendor (not included in this Sale), and will be sold with the right to use such water as is required for existing needs, and also subject to the right of the Vendor and others to use the water from such well. The approximate position of the well and the intended position of the pipeline are shown on the Plan.

This Lot is also sold subject to a right of way to the cottages on the East as shown on the Plan.

Sale of the Somerset Arms in 1899

The Somerset Arms in 2005

become a free house once more and has been extended from its original L-shaped plan to form an excellent family pub.

This old road from Monmouth to Raglan was improved by the Turnpike Trustees in 1810 to replace:

> a twisting and narrow lane, in places worn very deep into the clay, similar to the lanes in the neighbourhood. The new highway was made on the track of the old one in some places, but most of it is an entirely new road

wrote Bradney in 1913.

On the side of this road at Mitchel Troy stands another abandoned hostelry – the former **Glen Trothy**. This was kept in the 1970s by Ron and Irene Mitton and offered 'Fully Licensed Accommodation' with a campsite adjoining. It appears that the hotel later became a bed and breakfast establishment and the camp site became a caravan park. Mitchel Troy

A 1970s advertisement for the Glen Trothy

132

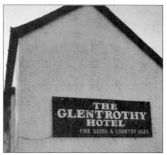

*The Glen Trothy Hotel in
2005 was closed by 2007*

is within two miles of Monmouth and is an attractive village where Troy House was formerly one of the seats of the Duke of Beaufort. In the 1860s the population of 387 were mainly employed in farming with some working as blacksmiths, wheelwrights, carpenters and stone masons. There was only one publican, John Lee, at the **Monmouthshire House**. This became the **Monmouth Inn**, kept by Philip Stead towards the end of the 19th century. No further records have been traced by the author.

Returning to the Monmouth to Trelleck road, a choice of lanes lead eastwards down to the Wye. At the Narth there was a popular but short-lived pub known as the **Trekkers**, which started life as a 'Log Cabin Style' holiday centre with a 'Private Members Licence' in the 1970s. New owners developed the log cabin into a pub, well remembered by the author as an enjoyable stop on the many walks in the area. The **Trekkers** has unfortunately been closed due to insurance problems and is still closed in 2007. From the Narth a delightful network of paths lead through the Whitebrook valley which enjoys an industrial past.

In the early 20th century T.A. Davies recounted a tale associated with the Narth. It involved a woman and a stranger who were flying around the Narth on

A 1975 advertisement for the Trekkers

133

The Trekkers functioned as a log cabin holiday centre and became a pub for a short length of time before closing

magical sticks. They flew to a country mansion and, after helping themselves to a good supper in the kitchen, pointed their sticks to the wine cellars below. He then wrote 'Drinking too much they got fuddled, and when they tried to get out they bumped their heads against the ceiling, roused the occupants, and were taken prisoner'. In those days burglary

The Crown at Whitebrook in 2005

meant hanging, but due to their witchery they avoided the hangman's noose.

In 1994 Heather and Jon Hurley wrote the following in their book *The Wye Valley Walk*:

> At Whitebrook, wire making was carried out between 1606 and 1720. From about 1760 papermills named Fernside, Sunnyside, Clearwater, Wye Valley and the Glyn were established along the busy stream, its crystal clear water being an essential ingredient in the making of paper. The finished article was transported from Whitebrook in barges along the Wye to Bristol. The industry continued until the end of the 19th century, when the mills were

gradually converted into dwellings. With their overgrown ponds they are now a picturesque sight.

At Whitebrook the existing **Crown** is easily recognised and found by following its signs. As a recommended restaurant 'Serving the finest cuisine, on a par with many of London's best restaurants, the Crown provides comfortable surroundings, with a warm welcome and attentive service from the proprietors'. The **Crown** has recently reopened after extensive refurbishment and bears no resemblance to its modest origins as a beer house run by the Seawards in the 1860s and '70s, before the Ricketts kept the pub to the turn of the century.

The one-time Bell in 2005

More difficult to locate at a minor junction in Whitebrook is the former **Bell** near the Baptist chapel. It was established as an inn before 1840, and was kept by John Morgan, a miller, in 1871 before George Brown took over the licence at the beginning of the 20th century. He was followed by the Reynolds and Probert families until the **Bell** closed in the 1960s.

Charles Heath in the early 1820s wrote an attractive introduction to the riverside village of Llandogo:

> from a stand on the summit of the path above the river, we enjoy the best view of this curious settlement. The river makes a fine curve, whose right screen is formed by a very extensive and lofty hill, every part of which is studded with cottages, from within a few yards of the Wye to the utmost summit of the rise. These dwellings are surrounded by abundance of the choicest fruit trees, which produce a great quantity of cider in a favourable season, while valuable herds of fine cattle are grazing in the vale below.

Since the building of the Wye Valley road and the construction of Bigsweir Bridge after the Road Act of 1824, Llandogo has become more accessible from both sides of the river by vehicle or on foot. Until that date 'most of the carrying of merchandise to and from Monmouth was by means of barges' wrote Bradney in 1913. He added 'There was at one time a

The Sloop in 2005

considerable traffic carried by ships locally called sloops, which carried timber and other products to Bristol. This trade has almost disappeared, but a few sloops are still employed'. The navigation on the lower Wye certainly declined after the opening of the Wye Valley Railway in 1876.

Llandogo of the 21st century has much to offer residents and visitors – a scenic situation, wonderful walks, a good village store, several bed and breakfast establishments and the **Sloop Inn**, which may be visited while following one of the printed *Village Walks* available from Brown's Stores. A leaflet explains that the **Sloop** was 'once a multi-purpose mill powered by water from the hillside streams and was regulated through the small hillside reservoirs'. The inn bears a weathered date stone understood to be either 1707 or 1770, and is named after the sloops and trows that once plied the river.

The **Sloop** was kept by Edwin Brisland in 1862, then Mary Brisland in 1871. They were followed by Alfred Williams, a master mariner who ran the inn during the 1880s and '90s. In 1879 Alfred was owner of the *Luna*, a 42-ton barge built at Bristol in 1842, and in 1886 the *George and Mary* – a 46-

The mosaic by Pat Yallop 'The Sloop's Resting Place in the 1890s'

ton trow – which, after Alfred's death in 1913, was left to rot on the river bank. During the 1920s Philip Crum took over the **Sloop Inn** before retiring to Coedithel Farm, and during the 1930s John Overs was the publican at the time when Llandogo was beginning to establish itself on the tourist map. There was Eddie's Tea Gardens at Brown's, a Holiday Fellowship centre at the Priory and many houses and cottages offering accommodation.

The **Sloop** had been purchased by the Stroud Brewery, which was taken over by West Country Breweries in 1962. As a Whitbread house the inn managed to remain open, and in 1990 was advertised as an award-winning 18th-century country inn:

Nestled in the heart of the Lower Wye Valley in the centre of this sleepy village [and offering] a comfortable mix of tradition and modern facilities. Spotlessly clean en suite character bedrooms, unpretentious food at realistic prices and a cheerful atmosphere.

Under new ownership in 2005, the **Sloop** free house was serving 'Wine and beer selection, including real ales, Traditional Bar Meals and Log Fire'. In the cosy bar a verse is displayed:

> The one and only village pub,
> Helpful staff, tasty grub.
> Excellent menu, beer and wine,
> Stop for a drink, rest and dine.
> Llandogo village is where we are,
> On your travels by foot or car.
> Once inside let's raise a toast!
> Ideal for walking, fishing or painting a scene,
> Near to the river and the Forest of Dean.

The **Ship** was another riverside inn dating from at least 1840, and associated with the Williams family of watermen. In 1862 it was kept by Thomas Williams a bargeman with a financial interest in the 35-ton barge called the *Joseph and Mary*. From around 1870 to 1890 Charles Gage occupied the **Ship** with his wife

*Above: Two 1970s
advertisements for the Old
Farmhouse Hotel
Right: The Hotel sign*

and family before George Williams took over at the end of the 19th century. It is now a dwelling known as The Old Ship and is reached by a footpath leading down to the Wye.

From Llandogo a steep and southerly ascent up to Cleddon leads past the former **Old Farmhouse**, which was an hotel in 1975 housed in a 16th-century farmhouse. Since 2000 the hotel has closed and the site has been redeveloped.

Further along the lane is Lion Cottage – the former **Red Lion** of 1862 kept by William Hopkins. It reappears in 1881 as **Bargins Road Lion Inn**, not to be confused with another **Red Lion** kept by

The Cleddon Lion

138

The one-time Lion Inn

Amos Hodges for a brief period. The **Lion** continued trading under Edwin Williams, Arthur Mapps and Charles Parker, and in 1929 it was valued at £800 by Wintle's Forest Brewery from Mitcheldean.

At Cleddon, the Wye Valley Walk passes the top of the Cleddon Falls, and provides a good view point. This is the start of a descent down a zigzag path laid out as a Tourist Path through the picturesque ravine in the mid-19th century. Charles Heath referred to the falls as the Clydden Shoots:

which when the springs are full, forms a beautiful cascade; while from the summit of the eminence, we command a very interesting view of the river and surrounding country.

Whereas Bradney over 100 years later wrote:

Here is one of the few water-falls in the county, the Cleddon brook falling precipitously down the ravine, and known as Cleddon Shoots.

Near the top of the shoots at Cleddon there was a beer house at Falls Cottage known as the **Three Horse Shoes**, or more rudely called the **Three Piss Pots**, but no documentation has been traced of this elusive inn. Another inn in this vicinity was the **Waterfall** mentioned in an 1840 deed as a:

Dwelling house situate at Llandogo, now or lately used as an Inn and known by the sign of the Waterfall Inn. Messuage adjoining with the gardens, orcharding and coppice wood planted with fruit trees situated at Llandogo, bounded on the east side by a place called the Green adjoining the road leading from Trelleck to Monmouth, on the north by a road leading from the

The one-time Three Horse Shoes in 2005

Green to the Mill Pond belonging to Philip Luff gent., on the west and south by land of John Gough and through which premises there is a carriage road to and from the said property of John Gough and through which water that runs from Cledian passes into the river Wye, formerly in possession of Joseph Madley, now in possession of Isaac Madley and Charles King his tenant.

The 'notorious poacher' (page 130) of 1810, who killed all the birds and sold them to Bristol, was Job Jones (or Williams) known as Job the Outlaw, who kept an inn at Cleddon. He also used to raid the deer in the Forest of Dean.

CHAPTER NINE

Trelleck, Llanishen & Devauden

From Monmouth, the B4293 leads south-east along a circuitous route high above the Wye Valley to the attractive and interesting village of Trelleck. It lies on a plateau almost surrounded by woodland where ancient lanes and tracks indicate a place of considerable importance. Trelleck once enjoyed the status of a town but, as Joseph Bradney wrote in 1913 'The town of Trelleck was formerly much larger than it is now, and similar to Grosmont, has become reduced till it is nothing more than a village'. Its history dates from the Bronze Age and has been followed through to medieval times when Trelleck became a large and important town, with 378 burgage plots recorded in 1288. Since then, several periods of conflict and strife have contributed to its decline into a rural village.

Trelleck was always reliant on road transport, being so far from the river Wye, but it was not until 1755 that 'the Road leading from Monnow Bridge aforesaid, by the Town of Trelleck, to the Crossway at the foot of Llanishen Common' was turnpiked by the Monmouth Trust, and was joined by a road from Chepstow via Devauden to Llanishen turnpiked in 1758. Although these roads were repaired and widened under the terms of the Act, it was necessary to improve 'the Road leading from the Cinder Hill aforesaid, at the Extremity of the said town of Monmouth, to Trelleck'.

When the Hon. John Byng rode through Trelleck in 1781 he described the following in his *Torrington Diaries*:

a storm of rain drove me into a publick house, with whose landlord I conversed about goats and the Welsh language: he told me that many goats were kept in the neighbourhood; that in his village they spoke English, but at the distance of 6 miles, understood it no more than my dog.

He continued to Trelleck Grange through open country with 'brush wood intermixed with rocks'.

In the 1820s Charles Heath noted:

> The cheerfulness of the village is much increased, by the carriages and equipages of the nobility and gentry passing thro' it, on their visit to Tintern and Chepstow, – the road to each of which places has been so much shortened and improved. ... Leaving the Inn, we proceed down the village to the blacksmith's shop, and making an abrupt turn to the left, enter of the new line of communication from hence to Tintern.

Trelleck is now a popular place to walk around and visit its unique sites of historical interest. In the churchyard is a preaching cross and a so-called Druid's Altar, and in the church itself is an unusual 17th-century sundial. Behind the church is a mound – the remains of a motte and bailey castle – and at the southern end of the village an archaeological dig is uncovering the 'Lost City of Trelleck' near the three Standing Stones and the Virtuous Well, where a sip of chalybeate spring water may perhaps be tasted before visiting the only remaining pub in this part of Trelleck.

Opposite the church is the **Lion Inn**, which the owner claims to date from 1580, although documentation only dates from 1829 when an auction was held 'At the Lion Inn Trelleck On Wednesday, the 13th May 1829'. Between 1842 and 1846 the **Lion** grew in stature to become the **Golden Lion** and was the meeting place of one of the Trelleck Friendly Societies. However, in 1856 the **Lion**, then described as the **White Lion,** was put up for sale.

Charles Jones was the 'victualler' in 1862 after which John Knight took over. Henry Jones aged 36 was at the Lion in 1881 with his young wife, two nieces and a servant. Alfred Jenkins purchased 'All that fully licensed public house known as the Lion Inn and Smithy situate in the Village of Trelleck' in 1912. It was later acquired by Wintle's Forest Brewery based at Mitcheldean

---

THE "WHITE LION" INN and PREMISES.

This is a neat, respectable little property, adjoining the Parsonage and opposite the Church in the Village of TRELLECK.

In the Occupation of Mr. Charles Jones.

THE HOUSE contains 4 Bed Rooms, Parlour, Kitchen, Back Kitchen, Bar, Brewhouse, Cellar, Dairy, &c.; and in the Yard, STABLE for 5 or 6 HORSES, Chaise House, Piggery, &c., with a good YARD, GARDEN, and Close of Meadow Land, as follows:—

No. on Plan.	Description.										Quantity. A. R. P.
257	Meadow	..	..	..	..	..	..	..	..	..	1 0 35
258	Ditto	..	..	..	..	..	..	..	..		0 3 15
							Total	..	..		2 0 10

This Lot is subject to a Burgage Rent of £1. 1s. 10d. Land Tax, 19s.

Sale of the White Lion at Trelleck in 1856

TRELLECK—LION INN.

ALL THAT fully licensed public house known as the Lion Inn and Smithy situate in the Village of Trelleck in the County of Monmouth TOGETHER with the garden and pasture land adjoining thereto and Numbered 48 on the Ordnance Survey Map of the said Parish AND ALSO ALL THAT piece of pasture land on the opposite side of the main road leading to the Lion Inn and Numbered 47 on the said Ordnance Survey Map All which said premises have an area of two acres one rood and two perches and are coloured pink on the plan drawn on a Deed dated the second day of December One thousand nine hundred and twelve and made between Charles William Tyler Frederick James Tyler and John Octavius Tyler of the one part and Alfred Jenkins of the other part ALSO ALL THAT piece or parcel of land containing by admeasurement eleven acres three roods and twenty-one perches or thereabouts situate in the said Parish of Trelleck in the County of Monmouth and Numbered 46 on the 2nd Edition 1901 of the Ordnance Survey Map of the said Parish and delineated on the plan drawn on a Deed dated the thirtieth day of November One thousand nine hundred and seventeen made between Henry Aviary Tipping of the one part and Alfred Jenkins of the other part and therein coloured pink all which said premises are now in the occupation of Albert John Canning as tenant.

Description of the Lion in the 1937 Wintles Brewery sale

The Lion at Trelleck in 2005

and was then taken over by Cheltenham Original Brewery Company in 1937 when Albert Canning was the tenant.

Little is known of the **Lion** when it eventually became a Whitbread pub, until it was purchased by Tom and Debbie Zsigo who converted the inn into a popular venue offering 'a fine range of real ales and ciders' in a cosy atmosphere boasting 'original oak beams and open fires' and its good food and great beers have meant that it has won a number of awards in the last few years.

Crown Inn Trelech

(Dave and Eve Jenkins)

BED AND BREAKFAST

(All Bedrooms with Hot and Cold Water, Centrally Heated)

BAR SNACKS   BUFFET   RECEPTIONS

Telephone Trelech 366

The Crown Inn is located on the old coaching road (B4293) between Chepstow and Monmouth, only 3 miles from the well-known Tintern Abbey which is the centre of the beautiful Wye Valley. Trellech is a peaceful village with its history dating back to the Roman Occupation of Britain.

The Crown Inn was built in 1684 on the site of an old Monastery. A feature of the main Lounge and Bar is its wonderful example of natural stonework complete with huge fireplaces which are now retained mainly for decorative purposes as all rooms are centrally heated.

A visit to 'The Crown' is always rewarding as it still holds a charm and certain character which is so often lost in the rush and bustle of modern living.

A 1970s advertisement for the Crown

On the opposite side of the road, and just south of Trelleck church, was the **Crown** which was housed in a building with an interior featuring two fireplaces suggesting a date of the 17th century. As a coaching inn it was ideally placed on the main thoroughfare between Monmouth and Chepstow, and offered ample room for horse-drawn vehicles to stop whilst drivers and passengers took refreshments.

In 1862, the **Crown** was kept by James Williams until around 1880 after which he was followed by a succession of landlords. When Dave and Eve Jenkins took over the inn in the 1970s it was offering 'Bar Snacks, Buffets, Receptions and Bed and Breakfast'. They advertised 'A visit to the Crown is always rewarding as it still holds a charm and certain character which is so often lost in the rush and bustle of modern living'. It was during the 1970s that the ownership of the area fronting the **Crown** came into dispute and was finally designated as a Village Green due to the efforts of the Friends of Trelleck. Despite this evocative advertisement, the **Crown** had declined by 1980 and remained empty for five years leaving the building 'derelict and in need of extensive attention'.

For a short time its future appeared to have been saved when Bob and Jane Evans, after months of refurbishment, re-opened the establishment as an up-market restaurant and renamed it the **Village Green**. But its 'Good Food, Good Wine & Good Beer' in comfortable surroundings was short lived and around 2004 the former old inn closed its doors once more.

Village Green Restaurant

TRELLECH

This recently restored and refurbished Old Coaching Inn has reopened as a very well-appointed Restaurant serving a very high standard of cuisine. Everything is prepared to order in our kitchen from fresh and mostly local produce.

If you get excited about really good food come and see us.

We do a set price 3-Course Lunch or a set price 5-Course Dinner, and a full À la Carte (menus change every week)

Ring Bob — Monmouth 860119

Open Tuesday-Saturday

The short-lived Village Green and restaurant, which closed its doors in 2004

The one-time New Mills, near which was the Mason's Arms

From Trelleck church a road leads north-east to the start of a right-of-way across Trelleck Common to New Mills – now a picturesque ruin of a former corn mill operated by John Robins in 1901. Near here, on a parcel of land 'bounded by the road leading to the New Mills through the Burnt Wood to White Brook', was the **Mason's Arms**. Erected by George Williams the younger, it was open in 1840 and in 1841 was insured as a public house for the not inconsiderable sum of £200, but after this date no record has been found.

An incident of 'Assault and Attempted Highway Robbery' near the New Mills was reported by the *Monmouth Beacon* in 1865: 'Thomas Cruse, an Irish hawker, was charged with assaulting and attempting to rob Herbert Williams, butcher, Whitebrook, near the new mills, Trelleck'. Apparently the butcher was on his way home between the two mills in Trelleck, when he was struck on the head, knocked into a ditch and beaten. At the hearing the prosecutor said Williams had previously met the hawker in a pub at Whitebrook, and explained that they were 'not very drunk' nor were they 'sober'. Although it was a weak case, the Irishman was charged with assault and attempted robbery, and 'The Bench inflicted a fine of 1s. and costs, believing the assault to be a very trifling one'.

A large portion of Trelleck belonging to the Duke of Beaufort was unenclosed until 1810 when an 'Act for Inclosing Land in the Parishes of Trelleck ...' was passed. This included Parkhouse, lying one-and-a-half miles south of the village, where John Williams, a beer retailer, opened his

The former Parkhouse Inn

Conservative Tavern in the early 1860s. Also known by the unwieldy name of the **Parkhouse Public Conservative Tavern**, it is not really surprising that it dropped the political element and from 1937, as the **Parkhouse**, it continued for a few more years under James Jones as landlord. The building is now a private dwelling and the stables, which were at one time the Stable Bar, have been incorporated into the present house.

Before leaving Trelleck, it is worth mentioning that, on the site of a forge recorded in 1746, a brewhouse was erected some time between 1809 and 1833 which was leased to William Williams in 1833 for £415. The property consisted of a dwelling house, garden, barn, brewhouse, stables, and a granary, and the brewhouse, stable and granary had previously formed two messuages. The brewhouse was in use for its original purpose until 1860, but by 1902 it had been converted into a shop, stores and blacksmith's forge. A malthouse, two dwellings, outbuildings, garden and a barn were conveyed for £200 in 1847, which may have been part of the same property. Although the location is unknown by the author, it is likely to have been sited on the sharp bend opposite the church, where a smithy is marked on the 1888 Ordnance Survey map.

Trelleck Grange was at one time a separate parish lying to the south of Trelleck village. The place acquired its name in the 12th century, after being granted to the monks of Tintern, who cleared and cultivated the land, making it the principal farm for supporting the abbey. The church, which once belonged to the abbey, was rebuilt in 1861 and stands in the midst of a cluster of farm buildings. Within a mile of here, and in a remote position, it is surprising to find an inn still open in 2006. This is the **Fountain**, one of three inns that Joyce Edmunds recorded in *Tales of Llanishen Parish*, the others being the **Vine Tree** and the **Ship**, the latter surviving as the name of a cottage.

The **Fountain**, according to the pub's history, dates back several centuries when it was an old drovers' inn. The local springs and wells would

Sale of the Fountain Inn in 1899

certainly have provided a good watering place for horses and cattle being driven between Monmouth and Chepstow along a route that avoided the toll roads. The **Fountain** was part of the Duke of Beaufort's estate, and in 1862 was kept by William Pugh, a beer retailer. He was followed by Isaac Beaven during the 1870s and '80s, and it was under his occupancy that an unfortunate case of manslaughter took place in 1888.

The *Monmouth Beacon* reported the 'Manslaughter at Trelleck' in all its intricacies and gory details. It concerned a fight between William Parker and James Pack, who was killed. At the inquest Isaac Beaven junior, a timberman staying with his father at the **Fountain**, gave evidence saying 'He believed Pack was drinking out of one pint and Parker out of another [before] they rushed out of the house ... and had a tussle', which led to the death of Pack. Obviously the tussle was far more serious than witnessed, because the doctor found Pack unconscious, badly bruised and cut with 'blood flowing from the nostrils, ears and mouth, also from a cut at the back of the head'. After a verdict of manslaughter, the deceased was buried at Trelleck the following Sunday. The funeral attracted over 300 people including members of the Trelleck Oddfellows, who paid tribute to their fellow member Park 'by dropping a laurel leaf into his grave'.

148

The Fountain Inn in 2005

With other inns belonging to the Duke of Beaufort, the **Fountain** was for sale in 1899. In 1901 John Harper ran the **Fountain** and some time after this date it passed to Wintle's Forest Brewery who recorded as it being in 'poor' condition in 1929. This was not helped by 'a disastrous fire in 1964 which almost ended the inn's life, but the old thick walls survived and after major re-building the inn re-opened for business two years later'. By 1975 the **Fountain** had become a 'French Restaurant' and in 1990 the '17th century Free House' was offering all the usual facilities including accommodation.

A 1975 advertisement for the Fountain

Llanishen and Devauden are both situated on the B4293 between Trelleck and Chepstow, on a route turnpiked by the Monmouth Trust in 1755 from 'Monnow Bridge aforesaid, by the town of Trelleck, to the Crossway at the foot of Llanishen Common', and by the Chepstow Trust from Chepstow via Devauden to Llanishen Cross in 1758. On the roadside is a long low range of buildings that forms the **Carpenters Arms**, which has served travellers from the past to the present day.

Above: The Carpenters Arms at Llanishen in 2005
Below: A 1990 advertisement for the inn

A mortgage of 1838 records that John Cobner, a yeoman, and his wife Hester occupied the **Carpenters Arms**, and in 1869 the property was still mortgaged. Isaac Thomas was the landlord during the 1880s, when Llanishen village had the services of a boot & shoemaker, a mason, sawyer, builder, blacksmith and a carpenter. The nearest railway station was three-and-a-half miles away at Llandenny on the Ross, Monmouth, Pontypool branch of the Great Western Railway. This had opened from Monmouth to Pontypool in 1857 and from Monmouth to Ross in 1873.

During the first half of the 20th century the '**Carpenters Arms Public**

The Carpenters Arms

LLANISHEN CHEPSTOW GWENT
TELEPHONE 0600 860405

WELL APPOINTED ACCOMMODATION
REAL ALE   REAL FOOD   REAL WINE

Real ales from the cask. A wide variety of home prepared food is always available with a carefully selected list of fine wines. Bedrooms are double or single with bathrooms en suite.

House' was run by Thomas James followed by successive publicans including Albert Howard and Annie Michael. In 1990 the inn was offering 'Real ale from the cask. A wide variety of home prepared food always available, with a carefully selection of fine wines' and at the start of the new millennium it was acknowledged as a 'Sporting Pub'.

From Llanishen, the Chepstow road passes Star Hill, where the views are panoramic, and the road signed to Raglan passes the **Star Inn** at Llanfihangel-Tor-Y-Mynydd. This was an old coaching inn that has survived into the 21st century, but its situation is just beyond the scope of this book.

From Star Hill the Chepstow road traverses Cobler's Plain to Devauden with its church, pub and village stores. Overlooking the green is the **Masons Arms**, known as a 'local' pub. It had

English and Welsh for the Carpenters sign

The Masons Arms at Devauden in 2005

151

been established before 1860 when John Haines, the publican had, according to Raymond Howell, gained a reputation for 'drunkenness, serving after hours and fighting with his customers'. Other pubs, probably beer houses, mentioned by Howells, were the former **Plough** replaced by the **Tredean Arms**, although no documentation has been found. Also mentioned in 1862 was the **Trout** which was kept by James Williams.

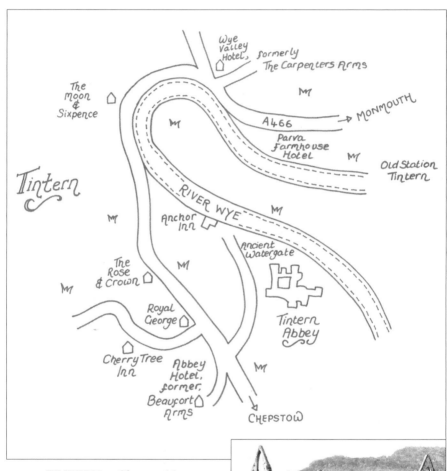

TINTERN – Chapter 10

Above: Pubs open in 2007

*Right: Tintern Abbey in the early
20th century*

CHAPTER TEN

Tintern & St. Arvans

Tintern is famous for the magnificent ruins of its 12th-century Cistercian Abbey, founded by Walter de Clare. The monks eventually became wealthy landowners, and during their years of prosperity extended and beautified the building standing so gracefully on the banks of the Wye. At the Dissolution the abbey was vandalised and left in a derelict state, but eventually attracted the attention of those seeking the Picturesque in the late 18th century. Apparently in 1756 a forward thinking man from Chepstow employed a hundred men to clear the abbey site of tumbling masonry and debris so that the ivy-clad ruins could be appreciated by the writers, artists and poets of that period. Since then Tintern Abbey has remained a popular tourist attraction with thousands of visitors every year exploring its cloisters, dormitory, nave, choir and chapter house.

In the second half of the 18th century three notable characters visited the abbey – the young William Turner whilst on a sketching tour, the poet William Wordsworth, who in 1796 wrote *Lines Composed a Few Miles above Tintern Abbey*, and the Hon. John Byng, who in 1781 recorded the following in his *Torrington Diaries*:

> Over this stile, and by this door I enter'd the abbey accompany'd by a boy who knew nothing, and by a very old man who had forgotten everything; but I kept him with me, as his venerable grey beard, and locks, added dignity to my thoughts; and I fancied him the hermit of the place.

Very sensibly he added:

> The way to enjoy Tintern Abbey properly, and at leisure, is to bring wines, cold meat, with corn for the horses; bread, beer, cyder and commonly salmon, may be had at the Beaufort Arms. [On the return from] these surveys, I dined in the kitchen of the alehouse on salmon, and tolerable ale.

With the decline of monastic life Tintern thrived as an industrial site with iron working, brass making, wire production and corn milling in the steeply wooded Angidy Valley. Its history can be followed step by step on a walk of 2½ miles called the Tintern Trail which starts from the **Anchor**, a riverside inn. From time immemorial the Wye has been a navigable river with goods transported up and down the waterway, but there was always trouble between the weir builders and the river traders. In 1334 the Abbot of Tintern heightened his weirs, which impeded boats carrying wine and victuals to Monmouth. Wine was transported from Bristol and Chepstow to go upstream, whilst cider, timber and agricultural produce went downstream from Hereford and the upper reaches of the river. Boats were made at many places on the river and in 1788 a sloop named *George and Elizabeth* was owned by a victualler from Tintern in 1788. In 1841, 23 inhabitants were employed in trades associated with the river, and 13 occupied inns and lodging houses.

Tintern relied more or less completely on the river to import and export goods because the main road that ran between Monmouth and Chepstow was on the high ground to the west via Trelleck. The construction of the Wye Valley road in the early 1820s was described by Charles Heath:

> In consequence of the New Line of communication between Tintern and Chepstow, a beautiful broad carriage road has been laid down, which has changed the former rough and indelicate foot-path, by the river side, which led to the West-door of the Abbey, from the Beaufort Arms Inn. ... It has been in contemplation to form a direct turnpike road, on the shore of the Wye, from Monmouth to Tintern Abbey, to join the road above mentioned.

The route from Monmouth to Redbrook had been turnpiked in 1755 by the Monmouth Trust, and was eventually extended to Tintern under the terms of the 1824 Road Act.

Transportation and communications were further improved in 1876 with the opening of the Wye Valley Railway which connected Monmouth to

A 1970s advertisement for the Parva Farm Guest House

154

The Parva Farmhouse Hotel in 2005

Chepstow. At Tintern a short branch line crossed the river to serve the wireworks. This former railway bridge now serves as a useful crossing for walkers and visitors exploring Tintern. The Wye Valley Railway was closed in 1964, but the station, signal box and sidings at Tintern have survived and have been converted into a pleasant picnic site, a display area and a tea room signposted off the valley road at the Old Station at Tintern. The old timetables show the journey by steam train from Tintern to Chepstow took under 20 minutes in 1876. Although there were only four return services a day, it was a faster, dryer and more comfortable trip than by foot or on horseback.

The Old Station at Tintern is a good starting point to investigate the past and present taverns of Tintern by initially following the Wye Valley Walk south along the river bank and past the dismantled railway bridge to St. Michael's church at Tintern Parva. Just beyond the churchyard is the **Parva Farmhouse**, a licensed hotel and restaurant described by the *Guardian* in 2003 as:

> [A] seventeenth-century stone farmhouse next to a small church, surrounded by wooded hillsides and overlooking the River Wye. Beamed lounge, inglenook fireplaces, leather chesterfield sofas and friendly.

The Carpenters about 1900. It eventually became the Wye Valley Hotel

The restaurant served unpretentious fare and the wine list included Monnow wine from Monmouth. The original Parva Farm was converted into a guest house during the second half of the 20th century, and in 1975 was described as a 'farmhouse and cottage annex dating from [the] 15th century'. Since then the buildings have been joined together but extended and still display an old AA sign.

Opposite **Parva Farmhouse**, and gracing a sharp bend on the main road, is the **Wye Valley Hotel**. It emerged from the original **Carpenters Arms**, a modest establishment that was kept by Mary Marsh in 1835 and then by various members of the Brown family until the end of the century. Wintle's Forest Brewery acquired the premises between 1923 and 1929 and renamed it the **Wye Valley Hotel** with David Jones as tenant. When Wintle's brewery and licensed premises were taken over by the Cheltenham Original Brewery in 1937 the inn was still occupied by David Jones. In 1975 the **Wye Valley Hotel** was described as a 'Fully Licensed Free House' offering accommodation and a restaurant.

To the right of the **Wye Valley Hotel** is the entrance to Parva Farm Vineyard which was planted with German vine types in 1979. The establishment welcomes visitors to tour the vineyard and taste their award-winning wines. Wine producers of the United Kingdom often claim that the Romans first planted vineyards in this country, but there is little evidence to

TINTERN.—WYE VALLEY HOTEL.

ALL THAT messuage or public house formerly known as The Carpenters Arms but now called and known as The Wye Valley Hotel with the site thereof and the outbuildings garden orchard and land thereto adjoining and belonging situate in the Parish of Tintern Parva in the County of Monmouth now in the occupation of David Perkins Jones as tenant.

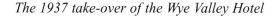

The 1937 take-over of the Wye Valley Hotel

The Wye Valley Hotel in 2005

support this theory However, in medieval times it is known that the monks made wines for the celebration of Mass.

Overlooking one of the Wye's long meanders at Tintern is the **Moon and Sixpence**, a pub in an 18th-century building which opened its doors as the **Mason's Arms** in the mid-19th century when it was run by William Price. There was a succession of landlords including one Alfred Watkins in 1937 (not the famous Herefordian who died in 1935), before it was renamed the **Moon and Sixpence**. The name was changed in favour of the 1919 novel by Somerset Maughan – *The Moon and Sixpence* — when the author visited the pub. The book was inspired by Maughan's visit to Tahiti. The story is about an Englishman, Strickland, who left his wife and

Above: Interior of the Moon and Sixpence in the 1970s
Below: A 1970s advertisement for the inn

A Fully Licensed Free House with an Old World Atmosphere

THE MOON & SIXPENCE

TINTERN, Nr. CHEPSTOW, Mon.

Snacks - Luncheons - Dinners

A La Carte Menu   Supper Licence

(Roast Aylesbury Duckling a speciality)

ADVANCE BOOKING ADVISABLE
Telephone : TINTERN 284

Under Personal Supervision of
Mrs. L. M. FLOWERS and PAMELA

stockbroker job to end his life in a leper's hut. The story was made into a film in 1943. In 1965 the inn was described as 'A Fully Licensed Free House with an Old World Atmosphere [under the] Personal Supervision of Mrs. L.M. Flowers and Pamela' who served 'Roast Aylesbury Duckling' as their speciality. These two women were still running the **Moon and Sixpence** a decade later, but had added a 'choice selection of wines and spirits' to their menu. In 1990 the bar offered 'Real Ale and Fresh Wye Salmon' which was enjoyed in front of the interior Trout Pond formed by a natural spring.

158

The Moon and Sixpence in 2005

Also in an enviable position is the **Rose and Crown**, which has been extended since the 18th century. David Waugh kept the inn in 1835 followed by the Charles family who ran the premises from the 1840s to the 1860s. Josiah Woolley was the proprietor in 1880 when the **Rose and Crown Hotel** became a 'Family, Commercial and Posting House'. At this date the hotel was the meeting place of a Tintern Friendly Society with the society's room still known today as the Club Room.

The **Rose and Crown** was one of many inns owned by the Duke of Beaufort and was put up for sale as a 'well-known house' in 1899 when W.J. Rogers Ltd. from Bristol was renting the property for £24 a year and sub-

Rose and Crown Hotel,

TINTERN ABBEY.

FAMILY COMMERCIAL

AND

POSTING HOUSE.

Wines and Spirits of the Best Quality.

CONVEYANCES MEET ALL TRAINS.

POSTING IN ALL ITS BRANCHES.

JOSIAH WOOLLEY,

PROPRIETOR.

The Rose and Crown in the 1880s

THE "ROSE & CROWN," TINTERN.

(FREEHOLD.)

A well-known House, delightfully situate on the Main Road, from Chepstow to Monmouth, overlooking the River Wye, and the Richly Wooded Hills beyond. It comprises

Tiled Hall, with Glazed Doors, leading to Coffee Room, Sitting Room, Large Excursion Room 22 ft. 6 in. by 22 ft., Bar Parlour, and Extensive Cellarage, Kitchen, Back Kitchen, Pantry, and above are Sitting Rooms and Eight Bed Rooms ; at Rear is a Lavatory.

At end is the Stable Yard, in which are Stable for Four Horses and Coach House.

Attached are extensive Terraced Gardens and Orchard, rising high above the Valley, and having frontages of about 143 and 250 feet to the Main Road, part of which could be profitably utilized for the erection of one or more Villas.

Also Two Strips of River frontage with Landing immediately opposite, and lying between the Main Road and River Wye.

PARTICULARS OF THE LANDS.

No. on Ordnance Plan	Description.	Quantity.			Remarks.
	TINTERN PARISH.	A.	R.	P.	
259	Garden...	0	1	27	
260	Orchard	0	1	28	
261	House buildings, &c.	0	1	16	
Pt. 262	River Frontage	0	0	4	
	TOTAL ACRES	1	0	35	

Let to W. J. ROGERS, Ltd., Bristol, for a Term of 40 Years, from Michaelmas, 1897, at a Rent of **£24** a Year, and Sub-let to Mrs. CHAMBERLAIN, at Rents amounting to **£58**, a large sum having been spent on the Premises since the Lease was granted.

Tenants paying Land Tax, **14s. 9d.** Tithe, **4s. 6d.**

NOTE.—This House is supplied with water by pipes from a Tank on land belonging to the Vendor (not included in this Sale), and will be sold with the right to use such water as is required for existing needs. This Lot is also sold subject to any Easement now existing for the pipeline carrying water from the same tank to Ashweir House bounded by this Lot and the road, and also to the right of the Vendor and others to use the water from such tank. The approximate positions of the tank and of pipelines supplying the "Rose and Crown" and Ashweir House are shown on the Plan. It is believed that there are separate pipelines from the tank for each supply, but it may be that the supply to both houses is conducted for part of the distance by means of one pipeline and subsequently duplicated for the purpose of carrying the supply to each house.

Sale details of the Rose and Crown in 1899

letting it to Mrs. Chamberlain for £58. At that time the pub consisted of a bar parlour, a coffee room, and a large excursion room with two sitting rooms, eight bedrooms, kitchens, extensive cellarage, a coach house, stabling for four horses and a river frontage with a landing stage. The **Rose and Crown Hotel** continued to attract business, especially tourists and cyclists in the 1920s. A few decades later it was advertised as a fully licensed inn, which it still was in 2006 with a reputation for Welsh beef steaks.

The **Royal George** stands on the corner of the Chepstow and Trelleck roads, and according to the pub's history was the iron master's house in the late 17th century when the Mineral and Battery Works were established to manufacture wire. Later it became an inn on the old pack horse trail known as Porthcasseg (the Pony Way) and developed into a coaching inn after the construction of the Wye Valley road in the 1820s. Its name probably dates from one of the royal Georges of the 18th or early 19th centuries, having acquired the **Royal George** sign by 1835 when David Evans was the innkeeper. By 1899 it had been elevated to a hotel which was sold as 'An Old Established Well-Placed Hotel'.

The Rose and Crown in 2005

The Royal George in 2005

161

Sale of the Royal George in 1899

In the 1920s the **Royal George** was catering for large and small parties visiting the Wye Valley and was eventually taken over by Trust Houses Ltd. They offered a 'Single Room, Bath & B'fast' for 7s. 6d. in 1939 in the hotel that had by then been extended. The **George** was still a Trust House in the 1950s, but since then it has become a Best Western hotel serving the 'best of local Welsh produce with a fine international wine list'.

Beyond the **George,** the Trelleck road leads up the steeply wooded Angidy Valley where the majority of Tintern's forges, furnaces and mills associated with the wire works were situated. Bradney in 1913 wrote:

> The site of the ancient works can be seen up the picturesque valley down which the Angidy brook, diverted into several ponds, descends rapidly from Pont-Seison (the Englishmen's bridge), perhaps so called from having been erected by English workmen, to the river Wye. Many cottages, a large number uninhabited, remain, and among them is a large house known as Gwyn.

Amongst these cottages is the **Cherry Tree**, an unusual premises operating over a basement shop, which can be accessed from the upper or lower roads from Tintern. Samuel Waite was a long-serving innkeeper of the **Cherry Tree** from 1860 until its sale in 1899 at which time he was only paying £1 rent a year. The sale particulars describe the inn as a stone and tiled house with two rooms on the ground floor and three rooms above, with a cellar, kitchen store house, cart shed, stable and garden.

The Delafield Brewery from Abergavenny acquired the property and in 1916 agreed to let the **Cherry Tree Inn** to Walter Goodman at an annual rent of £10. In 1965 the inn had already started to serve Hancocks Fine Beers, which were still available in 2006 when Wye Valley Butty Bach, Hereford Pale Ale, Cottage Brewery, Archers and many other real ales were available together with Bulmers and Thatchers ciders and a choice of wines from Torres to Penfold.

FULLY-LICENSED FREEHOLD AND TITHE FREE PUBLIC HOUSE,

KNOWN AS THE

" CHERRY TREE, "

Situate in the Parish of Chapel Hill, having entrances from both Upper and Lower Roads from Tintern to Pontysaison.

THE STONE-BUILT AND TILED HOUSE

CONTAINS

TWO ROOMS ON THE GROUND FLOOR AND THREE BED-ROOMS OVER.

At rear are Cellar, Back-kitchen, and Store House all opening from a paved yard. Beyond are two Bay Stone and tiled Cart Shed, Stable and Garden.

It is part of No. **137** on Ordnance Plan, and contains about

29 Perches.

Sale of the Cherry Tree in 1899

The Cherry Tree sign

The Cherry Tree

Further up the Angidy Valley a recent housing development has been built on the site of the former **Globe**, which was kept by Thomas Higley in 1862 and later by Frank Wheeler. According to a local resident it was closed around 1906 – this would have been after the wire works and tinplate works were closed in 1900 with its plant and machinery sold in 1901. A mile further up the valley, the ponds and dams of earlier industries including the ironworks were excavated by Gwent County Council in the late 1970s to reveal the layout of the buildings.

At Pont y Saeson (as spelt on the 1900 Ordnance Survey map) there was the **Pontsaison Cross Inn**, which hosted a Friendly Society and from the 1840s to at least 1880 was run by William Duffield as a cider house.

The **Abbey** has regretfully lost its original appellation – the **Beaufort Arms** – named after the local landowner. It was established as an inn some time before James Fishe was recorded there in 1763. The inn was mentioned by John Byng in his *Torrington Diaries* of 1781, whilst in the 1820s Charles Heath from Monmouth had plenty to tell his fellow travellers:

> Should fatigue take precedence of the reader's curiosity, he will find the Beaufort Arms, a very neat and comfortable Inn, kept by Mr. Mitchel, who has the care of the Abbey. If a party by water,– while the company are

MRS. C. EVANS,

'BEAUFORT ARMS'

COTTAGE HOTEL,

ABBEY, TINTERN.

Families and Tourists will find every comfort of a home in this romantic Hotel, which is delightfully situated close to the Abbey, and has a commanding view of the River Wye.

WINES, SPIRITS, CIDER, and MALT LIQUORS of the Best Quality.

An 1862 advertisement for the Beaufort Hotel – now the Abbey Hotel

Past and present officials of the Wye Valley Otter Hunt at the Beaufort Arms in 1936

viewing the Abbey, Mrs. Mitchel will provide any refreshments they may think proper to order ready on their return to the Inn. ... The larder at the Inn is at all times well supplied, – and Mrs. Mitchel will feel a pleasure in providing the entertainment. The house has been fitted up in a neat and commodious manner; several rooms have been added, furnished with new beds and bedding; and a fresh stock of new liquors laid in their cellars; it being their first wish to show every possible attention to the accommodation.

Coaches still took tourists from Chepstow up the Wye Valley in 1880 even though the railway had opened

John Brown took over the **Beaufort Arms** followed by Catherine Evans in the 1860s and '70s. She was offering 'Families and Tourists every comfort of a home in this Romantic Hotel' with 'Wine, Spirits, Cider and Malt Liquors of the Best Quality'. Towards the end of the 19th century the Garretts of the Beaufort Arms in Chepstow were the proprietors, and were still there in the 1920s when the **Beaufort** was awarded AA and RAC recommendations as an hotel. It was taken over by John Watts Hotels some time before 1948 and was later acquired by Embassy Hotels. In 2002 it was completely restored and renamed the **Abbey Hotel**.

The old coach road from Chepstow led to the ferry crossing over the Wye at Tintern, where two hostelries offered rest and refreshments to passengers waiting for the ferry. One was the **Ship**, which was a modest beerhouse in 1835 kept by William Tamplin, a shipwright who was probably related to the Tamplin family of mariners, barge owners and shipwrights who were based at Wilton and Chepstow in the late 18th century. From around 1884 John Wheeler took over the **Ship** from his father-in-law, and his family continued to live there until it was demolished in the early

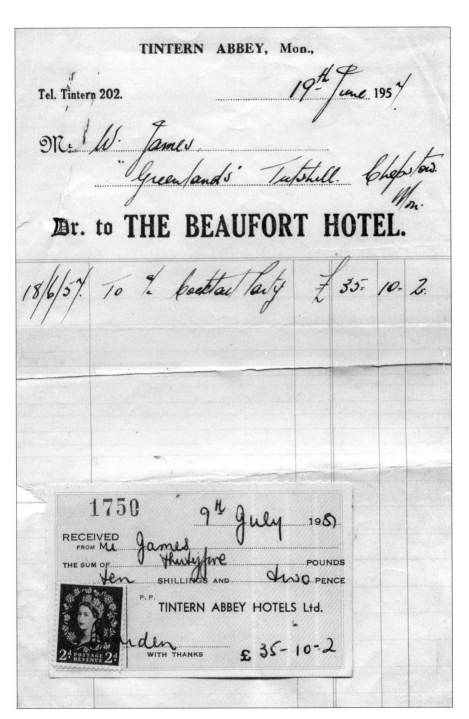

A rather expensive cocktail party at the Beaufort Hotel in 1957

Top: Inside the Beaufort in the 1920s
Bottom: The Beaufort – now the Abbey Hotel – in 2005

THE OLD ESTABLISHED FULLY-LICENSED RIVERSIDE INN

(FREEHOLD),

On the Banks of the Wye, and formerly the River Entrance to the Abbey, known as the

" ANCHOR " INN,

TINTERN.

Opposite the Ferry, and in the immediate vicinity of the Beautiful Ruins of **TINTERN ABBEY.** Well adapted for catering for River Parties and Sightseers visiting the celebrated Ruins.

The House, which stands on the Right Bank of the Wye, and faces the river, is approached through an ivy-clad archway and contains :—

ON THE GROUND FLOOR—Sitting Room overlooking the Wye, Smoke Room with side entrance, Bar, Tap Room Back Kitchen and Cellar.

ON THE FIRST FLOOR—Three Bed Rooms.

AT REAR—Cyder Mill and Cellar, with Stores over.

Attached is large Orchard and Garden, and at side is a Lawn suitable for outdoor refreshments. All situate in the Parish of Chapel Hill, and numbered 201 and 202 on Ordnance Plan,
CONTAINING ABOUT

3 Roods and 3 Perches.

Let to Mr. JOHN BROWN, on a Yearly Michaelmas Tenancy, with a Detached Stable not included in this Sale, at a Rent of **£18 per Annum,** and **£17 15s.** is the Rent apportioned on this Lot.

Above: Sale of the Anchor Inn in 1899

Left: The old cider mill at the Anchor Inn is still there on display

20th century. Following the demolition 'The foundation of walls on the opposite side of the road leading to the Abbey entrance were discovered on the removal of an old Inn'.

The **Anchor** stands adjacent to the ferry crossing, but the ferry ceased to operate after the First World War when the slipway was filled in. However, the remains of the Abbey's Water Gate can still be identified. In 1842 the **Anchor** was a beerhouse and shop kept by William Bowen who was followed by several other tenants until John Brown, who was renting the premises from the Beaufort Estate when it was sold in 1899. From the 1920s to the 1950s the **Anchor** was 'Noted for Salmon Teas' and 'Fresh Wye Salmon'.

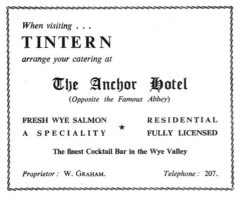

Advertising changes.
Top: 1925; Bottom: 1951

It was at Christmas in 2000 that a 'disastrous flood and landslip' due to heavy rain caused about £30,000 of damage to the **Anchor Inn**. Carpets were ruined and 154 gallons of beer 'had to be thrown away because it had become out-of-date by the time the pub reopened again'. All Christmas and Millennium parties had to be cancelled, and because the disaster happened over the holiday, the repairs and cleaning up were delayed, but according to the local press the pub reopened eleven days later in a 'sparkling and pristine' condition.

The **New Inn** and **King's Head** of 1842 were kept respectively by William Watkins and John Morgan, but were at premises still unknown to the author. Judith Russell in her *Tintern's Story* also lists a **Butcher's Arms**, which may have been run by one of the beer retailers of the 1840s when John Roberts was the principal maltster.

As Tintern moved from industry to tourism, a number of refreshment rooms, tea and coffee taverns and temperance hotels were established to satisfy the more temperate drinker. Even so, out of the fourteen licensed premises listed in Tintern, eight are still flourishing, which seems to show a greater percentage of survival as compared with other towns and villages.

In 1862 St. Arvans was:

a parish and pleasant village, bounded on the north-east by the river Wye, situated about 2 miles north-north-west of Chepstow, and about the same distance from Tintern. Wyndcliffe is a lofty eminence overlooking the Monmouth road, and commanding an extensive view of Monmouthshire and the adjoining counties, also of the rivers Wye and Severn. In the parish are the remains of two ancient chapels, dedicated respectively to St. Lawrence and St. Kingsmark. The living of St. Arvans is a perpetual curacy, in the gift of the Duke of Beaufort, and at present held by the Rev. W.F. Cresswell.

The Anchor Inn at Tintern in 2005

There is also an Independent Chapel and a National School. Population in 1851, 933. The Piercefield Hotel, a well conducted establishment, is most conveniently situated and visitors to this romantic neighbourhood, being close to the far-famed walks of Piercefield, admission to which can be obtained of the landlord of the above hotel.

In 1862 St. Arvans had two beer retailers, a plasterer and tiler, a school mistress, a hotel keeper, a grocer, blacksmith, boot and shoemaker, wheelwright and carpenter, a parish clerk, a plumber, painter and glazier, a butcher, a lime burner, three farmers and a cattle dealer. According to Raymond Howell in *Fedw Villages* of 1985 the **Piercefield** opened in 1825. It was kept by Joseph Dutfield in 1835, followed by Richard Harrison, a dealer in 'Foreign Wines and Spirits', in 1850. The property was sold in 1854 with its bar, parlour, sitting room, kitchen and its stabling, coach house and cider mill. In 1880 'A Four Horse Coach' from Chepstow called daily at the **Piercefield** for one hour to allow tourists to view the magnificent scenery at the Wyndcliff and Moss Cottage before a further two hours were allowed at Tintern, all for the return fare of 2s. 6d.

During the early 20th century Joseph Huxley was a long-term tenant of the **Piercefield**, after which it was acquired by the Stroud Brewery who sold it to West Country Breweries in 1962. The Gloucester Caving Club met at the inn when they were exploring the Otters Hole – one of the caves that was discovered in the cliffs between St. Arvans and Chepstow. The **Piercefield** in

171

Monmouthshire.

IN THE PARISH OF
St. ARVANS.

TO BE SOLD BY AUCTION,
BY
Mr. John Davis,

AT THE GEORGE HOTEL, CHEPSTOW,

On Thursday, the 7th day of January, 1869,

At THREE o'Clock P.M. (Subject to such Conditions as shall be then produced)

THE UNDERMENTIONED

Eligible Freehold Property,

VIZ:—ALL THAT

MESSUAGE

(now used as a Licensed Beerhouse)

WITH A

COTTAGE under the same Roof,

and the Brewhouse and other convenient Out-offices, together with the Carpenter's and Smith's Shops and Yards thereunto adjoining, and the very productive Garden in the rear of the said premises, situate in the Village of St. Arvans, and being Nos. 169, 171, 172, 173, & 173a. on the Tithe Map and Apportionment of the said Parish, and containing together by admeasurement 3r. 16p. (more or less) now in the respective occupations of Mr. John Hill, Mrs. Catherine Dodds, and Mr. William Howell.

These Premises front the Turnpike Road, and are bounded by Lands of Henry Clay, Esq., The Representatives of the late Mrs. Bainbridge, and The Representatives of Mr. Morgan Jones, and the whole offers a very desirable investment.

Mr John Hill will shew the Property, and further particulars may be had of

The Auctioneer, or of Messrs. BALDWYN & MORGAN,
Ash Cottage, Chepstow.   SOLICITORS, CHEPSTOW.

GRIFFITHS, PRINTER & BOOKSELLER, BEAUFORT SQUARE, CHEPSROW.

The sale of an unnamed beer house in St. Arvans in 1869

1990 was a 'Beefeater Steak House' and attracted many race-goers from Chepstow Racecourse. By 2006 it had become a Brains Brewery pub offering a range of speciality beers with barbeques on summer race days.

From the Wynd Cliff, the Wye Valley Walk leads from the lofty cliffs, which rise to over 700 feet, down to the Lower Wynd Cliff and then through Piercefield's 'Picturesque Walk' laid out by Valentine Morris in the 18th century. The leafy path winds above the Wye past sites named the Cold Bath, the Giant's Cave, the Grotto, the Platform and the Alcove, offering many outstanding views before reaching Chepstow. In 1828 Moss Cottage was built at the bottom of the 365 steps which joins the Upper and Lower Wynd Cliff. This was a thatched cottage where visitors could take tea and refreshments and in 1925 was run by Ellen Wetson, but no record has been found of alcoholic drinks being served. There is a suggestion by Raymond Howell that **Wyndcliffe House** was an inn during the 19th century. It may have been associated with George Flowers, a beer retailer in the 1870s, before the house was converted into apartments.

At St. Arvans there was an earlier inn known as the **Squirrel** which was recorded by Charles Heath:

> at the upper end of the village of St Arvans, a few hundred yards from the termination of these Walks, – is an Inn, called the Squirrel, whose carriages and horses can be taken care of, during their stay at Persfield; – and should they afterwards wish to extend their excursion to Tintern, – two miles and a half, – there is a good driving road to the Abbey; and a New line of communication with it is now laid down.

The **Squirrel** appears to have been replaced by the **Piercefield**, as was another beer house known as the **Globe**. A sale poster of 1869 may relate to the **Globe**, describing it as:

> All That Messuage now used as a Licensed Beerhouse with a Cottage under the same Roof, and the Brewhouse and other convenient Out-offices, together with the Carpenter's and Smith's Shops and Yards thereunto adjoining, and the very productive Garden.

The premises fronted the turnpike road and were occupied by John Hill, Catherine Dodds and William Howell.

The Chepstow Racecourse opened in 1926 on a site:

> within easy access of the big industrial centres of South Wales and the big Berkshire and Wiltshire training establishments, and owing to the facilities promised by the Great Western Railway Company is easily reached from Newmarket ... The members' stand provides large luncheon and refreshment rooms,

which no doubt were licensed as they are today.

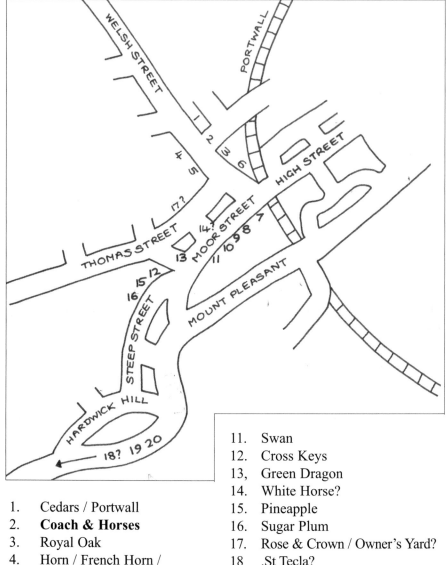

1. Cedars / Portwall
2. **Coach & Horses**
3. Royal Oak
4. Horn / French Horn /
   Squirrel
5. **King's Head**
6. Bear
7. **George**
8. Greyhound/Bell
9. Mitre
10. Queen's Head

11. Swan
12. Cross Keys
13, Green Dragon
14. White Horse?
15. Pineapple
16. Sugar Plum
17. Rose & Crown / Owner's Yard?
18. .St Tecla?
19. **Two Brewers**
20. **Chepstow Hotel / Two Rivers /
    Old Course**

Uncertain position
    Lower George?

Bold open in 2007

CHEPSTOW – Chapter 11: Welsh Street, Moor Street & Steep Street

CHAPTER ELEVEN

Chepstow:
WELSH STREET, MOOR STREET & STEEP STREET

From Monmouth the Wye Valley road heads south and closely follows the river to the outskirts of Chepstow. At the Crossway Green roundabout, the old road leads into the town with its Norman castle, priory church, medieval town walls, and present day museum, library, shops and riverside gardens. From the Town Gate a choice of narrow streets leads steeply down to the riverside where the castle ruins overlook the Wye and provide a unique and dominating feature of the Wye Valley. Restaurants and cafés offer a variety of refreshments, but the surviving pubs only represent a small proportion of the many past inns and hostelries of Chepstow which have been researched from original sources by the author.

Separated from England by the river Wye, the Welsh town of Chepstow developed into an important market centre and riverside port. A Roman road crossed the Wye upstream from the present crossings, and the Normans built the castle, founded a Benedictine Priory and called the place *Striguil*. During the 13th century the town wall known as the Portwall was constructed and a market was established. Leyland in 1538 noted:

> The Towne of Chepstow hath been very strongly waulled as yet welle doth appere. The Waulles began at the Ende of the great Bridge over Wy, and so came to the Castel, the which yet standeth fayr and strong not far from the Ruin of the Bridge.

William Coxe approached Chepstow via the New Passage over the Severn in 1801, and wrote:

> Chepstow is seated in a deep hollow inclosed by impending hills, and occupies the side of a declivity shelving to the right bank of the Wy, which here bends in a semicircular form. From this position the approach to it from the

175

New Passage is extremely singular; at the distance of only a quarter of a mile, the masts of the shipping seem to rise in the midst of an immense stone quarry, of which the perpendicular cliffs of the Wy form the side, but not a single house can be distinguished. On reaching the brow of the eminence, the town suddenly appears shelving to the bank of the river, and a singular intermixture of buildings, vessels, cliffs, water, and wood is presented to view. A rapid descent through an old gothic gateway, which formed the entrance of the ancient town, to the market place, and from thence to the bridge over the Wy.

Chepstow town grew from its early Norman settlement alongside a road joining the castle and the priory, around the wide market square and down the narrow streets descending to the Wye crossing. The construction of the Portwall in the 13th century provided protection to the town, which could be accessed on the land side through the single Town Gate in the Portwall or across the Wye at the bottom of the town. The town's later development may be traced from maps and plans dating from the late 17th century showing its growth and expansion. The first breach in the Portwall was for the South Wales Railway which opened in 1852, then followed a large-scale demolition when the shipyard was constructed in 1917 and, late in the 20th century, further breaches for the inner relief road of 1988 and the Welsh Street car park.

Throughout the centuries Chepstow has been associated with wine, beer and cider served from its various taverns, inns and beer houses. In 1306 the price of ale from the borough was worth £20 *per annum*, and the lord, Roger Bigod, received 'from every tavern of a burgess so often as he brew, 32 gallons of good ale for 4d'. The Benedictine Priory probably had a vineyard with cellars later used as a bonded wine store, and it has been suggested that medieval cellars in the town and castle were used as taverns or wine stores. According to the Hon. John Byng in 1781 there were only two inns of note in Chepstow, the **Cranes** and the **Beaufort Arms**, although a few years later Charles Heath from Monmouth listed the **Beaufort Arms**, the **George** and the **Bell** as the principal coaching inns.

During the 19th century Bradney recorded that:

the main roads, which had previously been mere lanes, leading into Chepstow were widened, straightened and much improved, so that fast coaches could travel ... and the road from Crossway Green, which had formerly meandered through what is now Piercefield park, was made to St Arvans.

Today this 19th-century road is followed from St. Arvans to Crossway Green and along Welsh Street, past a site which was called the World's End in 1695 and marked on the 1801 map as 'House called Worlds End'.

The Cedars Hotel became the Portwall in the 1970s

Although shown as the first building on the outskirts of Chepstow, it does not appear to have been recorded as a public house. It was further along Welsh Street that the inns and pubs were sited.

Once past the entrance to Castle Dell, offering views of Chepstow's ruined castle, the first prominent building is Castle Court featuring a heavily glazed Jacobean-style front with a three-storey porch. This was the **Cedars Hotel**, in 1965 a fully licensed establishment offering 'Peaceful Luxury' with a cocktail bar and restaurant run by Mr. and Mrs. Bools. It was renamed the **Portwall** in the 1970s serving 'a wide range of beers, wines and spirits, to be supped in Scandinavian style'. Obviously this did not succeed as the premises was converted into a retirement home in 1984 and renamed Castle Court.

On the same side of Welsh Street is the **Coach and Horses,** claimed to date from the 16th century, but only recorded as a beer house until blossoming into the cosy **Coach and Horses** in the mid-19th century. Henry Hope was the landlord in 1862 followed by the exotically named Hezekiah Pask in 1871. Before 1937 the **Coach and Horses** was taken over by Arnold Perrett and Co., and when James Park was the licensee, the pub passed to the Cheltenham Original Breweries as:

All that messuage tenement dwellinghouse now and for some time past used as an Inn Alehouse or Victualling House and commonly called or known by the name or sign of the Coach and Horses. Together with the yard stable brewhouse outbuildings premises and appurtenances thereto adjoining.

A street party at the Coach and Horses

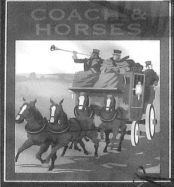
The Coach and Horses sign

The Coach and Horses in 2006 served Brains beer from their brewery in South Wales

On the same side of Welsh Street going towards the Town Gate was the **Royal Oak**, on or near the site of Coulters Wine Shop. William Fey was recorded as the licensee at the inn in 1858. It was conveyed from William Toye to William Phillips in 1873 and was taken over by the Stroud Brewery. In 1962 West Country Breweries acquired the Stroud Brewery and their licensed properties included the **Royal Oak**, which closed shortly afterwards. The wine shop was closed in 2007.

Horn Inn

Family & Commercial Hotel

WELSH STREET,
CHEPSTOW.

C.T.C. HOUSE.

Large or Small Parties Catered for.

SUITABLE ROOM WITH PIANO
FOR REHEARSALS.

Every Accommodation for Cyclists and Tourists.

MODERATE TERMS.

CLEMENT SMALLMAN,
PROPRIETOR.

The Horn or French Horn was once called the Squirrel

Almost opposite the former **Royal Oak** in Welsh Street was the **French Horn** of 1835 leased to Hannah Gwatkin. After the death of Hannah in 1842 the 'Messuage or tenement or Inn called the Horn situated in Welsh Street' was leased to John Morgan, who kept the attractive looking pub for a number of years, and was eventually followed by Ann Morgan. In 1905 Clement Smallman was the proprietor of the **Horn Family and Commercial Hotel**. He offered a 'Suitable Room with Piano for Rehearsals' and also 'Every Accommodation for Cyclists and Tourists'. Other tenants continued at the **Horn** before it was acquired by Arnold Perrett & Co. and taken over by Cheltenham Original Breweries in 1937. The conveyance referred to its earlier name, the **Squirrel**, 'but now and for many years past known and called by the sign of the Horn Inn or Public House Together with the stable and yard clubroom billiard room and garden'. Although the **Horn** did not

A 1925 Advertisement for the King's Head

survive after the 1960s, the
stone mounting block, which
once stood outside the pub,
has been preserved in a
shrunken form in Welsh
Street.

The **King's Head**, stands
on the corner of Welsh Street
and Thomas Street, and
Pevsner describes its façade
'with sweepingly arched
doorway flanked by broad,
segment-headed windows, in
concave surrounds'. It was
completely rebuilt after a fire
in 1907 and serves as an example of early 19th-century architecture. The
King's Head was a coaching inn and is claimed by the landlord to date from
the late 18th century. Daniel Baker ran the inn during the 1830s and a century

The King's Head in 2006

later R. Jones was the proprietor, probably before the Stroud Brewery took over the 'Inn in Welsh Street known as the King's Head Hotel with the skittle alley outbuildings and land' which then passed to West Country Breweries in 1962. In 2006 it was a Punch House keen 'to attract shoppers and workers in the town by offering the ideal venue for a relaxing drink'.

An 1862 advertisement for the George Hotel

The George before the 1896 fire

The 13th-century Town Gate forms the northern entrance into the town from Moor Street. It features a carriageway arch with a pedestrian passageway added at a later date, and is understood to have been rebuilt in 1524. In Moor Street there was an inn on each side of the Town Gate, the **Bear** and the existing **George**. The **Bear** was recorded in 1695 and an illustration in the National Library of Wales shows it was still open around 1800. The **George** has a long and fascinating history dating from the early 17th

The George Hotel,

CHEPSTOW.

Family and Commercial.

Centrally situated. Close to Town Gate, River and Railway Station.

LARGE ROOM CAPABLE OF DINING 100, AND ALSO SUITABLE
FOR MEETINGS, CONCERTS, etc.

HEADQUARTERS C.T.C.
AND R.A.O.B. . . .

GOOD BILLIARD TABLE.   TELEPHONE 0198 Nat

Terms moderate on application.

Within easy distance of Raglan Castle, Goodrich Castle, Tintern, Ross, Usk, Symonds Yat,
Speech House, and all parts of the Wye Valley.

MR. and MRS. PERKINS

take every care to make Visitors comfortable.

A 1905 advertisement for the George Hotel

182

century which is well documented in the booklet *The George and the Gate*, produced by the Chepstow Society in 1999. Tragically a fire in 1896 destroyed the earlier building; it was rebuilt in 1898 displaying a façade described by Pevsner as 'stark Neo-Tudor'.

According to the documents at Gwent Record Office, the **George** was leased to a widow and three merchants in 1798 from William Partridge of Goodrich – probably a member of the iron-making family. It was described as:

> All that messuage tenement or Inn by name or sign of the George Inn with yard, garden, orchard, brewhouse, outhouses and premises ... being near the Gateway in the town of Chepstow aforesaid having street called Moor Street in front thereof.

A further lease, made in 1810 from the same Partridge to James Price, is slightly misleading. It starts: 'All that messuage tenement or Inn commonly called the George situated in Moor Street' but also includes a coach house, yard, gardens and outbuildings, and also two stables with barns and yard with messuage or tenement situated in Welsh Street for 'many years last past have been in tenure or occupation of James Church'.

In 1835 John Clarke kept the **George** with coaches called the *Bath Coach* to Bath, the *Nimrod* to Raglan and Brecon and the *Accommodation* to Ross. This would have been a busy period for the inn with coaches arriving and departing nearly every day of the week. In 1849 Daniel Baker from the **King's Head** had taken over the running of the **George** and in 1859 John Parry James was the proprietor catering for 'Families, Tourists, and Commercial Gentlemen' with 'Posting in all its Branches – Lock-Up Coach House, Wines and Spirits of the Best Quality'. After the railway had opened J.P. James of the **George** ran a service of omnibuses to and from the trains

THE GEORGE HOTEL

FIRST-CLASS FAMILY AND
COMMERCIAL HOTEL

FIVE MINUTES WALK FROM STATION.

EXCELLENT CUISINE.   LISTED R.A.C. & A.A.**

Increased Accommodation recently added.
Hall for Banquets. Parties Catered for.
Garage Accommodation. Electric Light throughout.

MODERATE CHARGES.
For Tariff apply C. H. BRAMALL, Proprietor.

Telephone 365.   *Telegrams : George Hotel, Chepstow.*

The George sign   *A 1925 advertisement*

with 'Flys, Clarence, Phaetons Etc' for hire, and before the fire in 1896 J.H. Richards kept the **George Railway Hotel**. The devastating fire was reported in the *Chepstow Weekly Advertiser* as an 'Alarming Fire at Chepstow, Destruction of the George Hotel', and although the fire brigade was called in the middle of the night, there was a shortage of water to quell the flames. It appears that there was no loss of life as the residents and staff escaped down the back stairs, but the damage to the property and stock in trade insured respectively for £1,500 and £650 did not cover the total loss. However, the **George** was rebuilt, and in 1899 a notice in the *Chepstow Weekly Advertiser* informed the public that the Hotel was 'Now Open'.

In 1905 Mr. and Mrs. Perkins were taking 'every care to make Visitors comfortable' in the **George**, which could then accommodate 100 diners. The hotel became a Trust House by the 1950s and in 1998 was 'a traditional friendly hotel' with a bistro offering international dishes, and a bar serving traditional ales. The **George** was not alone – there was also a **Lower George** in 1668 recorded in Chepstow parish registers at an unknown site.

The George in 2006

184

The Greyhound on the right with the Town Gate and the George
in the distance in this 1920s postcard

The Greyhound, CHEPSTOW

Wines, Spirits and Ales
OF BEST QUALITY

PARTIES CATERED FOR.

Good Accommodation for Cyclists and Tourists.

NOTED HOUSE FOR
Godsell's Ales and Stouts.

JACK HUTCHINGS,
PROPRIETOR.

A 1905 advertisement for the Greyhound

The Beaufort Estate sale of the Greyhound in 1899

The Greyhound in 1930

The one-time Greyhound in 2000

From the Town Gate, Moor Street leads in a south-westerly direction towards the Newport Road and in the mid-19th century there was a line of pubs on the east side of the street. The **Greyhound** according to Bradney was 'anciently called the Bell and belonged in 1692 to Nathan Rogers' who in that year sold the inn to Giles Pope. His son mortgaged the property in 1738 when it was described as 'all that messuage ... called by the sign of the Bell, but now of the Greyhound'. By 1800 it was William Griffiths who owned the premises and in 1835 it was kept by John Clarke. Sarah Watkins was the landlady in 1849 when it was a meeting place of a Chepstow Friendly Society.

The Watkins family at the **Greyhound** were followed by Ann Barber who was the tenant in 1899 when the inn, as part of the Beaufort Estate, was for sale, and described in the particulars as a 'Fully-Licensed Freehold Tithe Free House' containing a tap room, bar, parlour, back kitchen and old brew house with six bedrooms on the upper two floors. From the double-boarded gates was a large yard with four stables, a store house, a slaughter house and a 'Stone and Tiled Smithy and Shoeing Forge and Stable'.

From 1901 John Hutchings was the proprietor offering 'Wines, Spirits and Ales of Best Quality, Good Accommodation for Cyclists and Tourists', and a 'Noted House for Godsell's Ales and Stouts'. The **Greyhound** was run by J.S. Burnell in 1925 as a 'Family and Commercial Hotel' and by E.T. Powell in 1937, well before the Stroud Brewery was acquired by West Country Breweries in 1962. About a decade later the **Greyhound** closed its doors for a final time.

The other pubs continuing this line up Moor Street included the **Mitre**, with a license that was transferred from John Barrett to Edwin Brisland in 1858, and where Laura Johnson served as the last licensee before it was demolished.

Next came the **Queen's Head,** housed in an attractive building that was for sale in 2006. This pub fared better than its neighbour. John Gardner and his family kept the place going from the 1850s to the 1880s, and after Arnold Perrett & Co. acquired the premises Harry Edwards was the publican in 1937 when it was taken over by the Cheltenham Original Brewery and presumably passed to Whitbread before closing a few years ago.

CHEPSTOW.—THE QUEEN'S HEAD INN.

ALL THAT messuage or Inn known as The Queen's Head situate at Chepstow in the County of Monmouth TOGETHER with the garden behind the same and all outbuildings and appurtenances thereunto belonging TOGETHER with the site thereof and the land occupied therewith.

Sale of the Queen's Head in 1937

The remaining former pub in this line-up was the **Swan**, recorded in 1722, which stood on the site of the Conservative Club before it was demolished in the 1870s.

On the opposite side and at the end of Moor Street were two inns – the **Green Dragon** and the **Cross Keys**. The latter, on the corner of Steep Street, had a short life during the mid-19th century when a stonemason

Above: The Queen's Head sign
Left: The inn was closed in 2006

The one-time Cross Keys in 2006

called Walter Griffiths lived there in the 1860s. The heraldic name usually refers to St. Peter, to whom Jesus said 'I will give unto thee the keys of the kingdom of heaven'. Another possibility is that it relates to being at a junction of roads, and not from its relationship with the church.

The **Green Dragon** was associated with the Chepstow Turnpike Trust, which was established in 1758 after an Act was passed for 'Repairing the Road from the Village of Magor to the Bridge-foot in the town of Chepstow'. Under the terms of the Act the trustees were empowered to erect gates and toll bars at convenient places where the tolls were to be collected. As the **Green Dragon** was situated at the junction of Moor Street with Steep Street a turnpike gate was erected there. Steep Street was the main road from Newport into the town until 1808 when it was replaced by the Mount Pleasant road. The **Green Dragon** had a succession of publicans throughout the 18th and 19th centuries and

The Green Dragon in 2000 at the end of its life as a pub

survived the 1960s, but unfortunately it then ceased to exist as a pub. However, in 2006 it still offered a delicious range of refreshments from a Good News type café called the Rainbow. The **Green Dragon** name is a fairly popular sign in the Welsh borders – it represents the Earl of Pembroke's coat of arms,

There was at least one other pub in Moor Street, which in 1824 was called the **White Horse**. An agreement of this date was made between William Davis and James Evans 'to give up possession of the house, gardens, buildings which he rents of Harriet Williams called the White Horse in Moor Street'. There is no further documentation of this inn, and it has been suggested that it was another name of the **Greyhound**. Beer retailers in Moor Street include Charles Hignell of 1859 and William Watkins of 1871. The **Boar's Head** and the **Crown and Thistle** in Moor Street and Welsh Street were listed by Ivor Waters.

From the southern end of Moor Street, the old and narrow Steep Street leads onto Hardwick Hill, but this narrow road was once known as Deadman's Lane –the main road leading out of the town towards Newport. Two inns with unusual names were recorded in Steep Street, the **Pineapple** and the almost unknown **Sugar Plum**.

The **Pineapple** was kept by George Thomas in 1859 followed by various publicans including Thomas Ireland and Eliza James before 1914

The Pineapple Inn in retirement:
Above: the old sign
Right: The building in 2006

The one-time Sugar Plum Inn

when Walter Goodman became the tenant of the Delafields Brewery in Abergavenny. The **Pineapple** was later taken over by Arnold Perrett & Co. and passed to the Cheltenham Original Brewery in 1937 as 'All that Messuage or tenement used as a Public House and called or known by the name of the Pine-Apple Inn with the yard stable piggery and outbuildings'. It closed shortly after this date but the name has been retained. The **Pineapple** is a pub name more commonly used since the fruit was introduced into this country during the 17th century. Some pubs called the **Pineapple** were often situated near fruit markets

190

where the fruit was for sale. The **Sugar Plum** sign was unique. The name applies to an oval-shaped sweet that has been made since the 17th century.

Thomas Street runs parallel to Welsh Street, and is now dominated by a supermarket and a busy bus station. This must have been a quieter street at one time with at least one pub known as the **Rose and Crown**. This appeared to have started life in the early 19th century as a beer house run by Sarah Mason, then Sarah Hill as the **Owner's Yard** associated with the 'Chepstow Free Gardeners Friendly Society' in 1862, although an earlier deed of 1847 records it as an 'Inn called the Rose and Crown belonging to Sarah Hill, widow' in Thomas Street. Sarah was still at the beer house in 1871, but by 1901 Giles Griffiths was the beer retailer.

Arnold Perrett & Co. acquired the **Rose and Crown**, and in 1937 when William Delaney was pulling the pints it was taken over by the Cheltenham Original Brewery. The conveyance makes interesting reading about a pub that no longer exists:

> All that messuage or dwellinghouse with the yard thereto adjoining and all outbuildings and appurtenances thereto belonging situate and known as the Rose and Crown Thomas Street Chepstow in the County of Monmouth. Together with the site thereof and the land occupied therewith And Also All That piece of land situate in Howells Court Thomas Street Chepstow aforesaid near to the said messuage or Public House upon which eight messuages cottages or tenements formerly stood. But subject to the right of the owners of the premises on the north-east side and their tenants of a footway and a way for horses waggons carts and all other carriages to pass and repass at all times in and through a certain passage under a part of the said dwellinghouse called the Rose & Crown to and from the said street called Thomas Street to and from a malthouse messuages and garden and other premises there situate. And subject also to the right (if any) of the owners of the five cottages in Owners Yard and their tenants to the use of the upper cistern in the same yar.

Arnold Perrett & Co had their Offices and Store in Albion Square, where a beer house of that name was kept by John Jeremy in 1849.

The remaining licensed premises in this chapter were and are in Newport Road and at Bulwark, which was a housing estate built as part of a First World War project to house the workers in the new National Shipyard at Chepstow. Bulwark is taken from the name of the Iron Age camp sited in this area. Many people are housed at the Bulwark, and it is surprising that only two pubs have been listed. One was the **St. Tecla**, once a Stroud Brewery pub that was open in 1951, taken over by West Country Breweries in 1962, and located at a site unknown to the author. The other

The Two Brewers in 2001

The Two Rivers is now the Chepstow Hotel

is the **Two Brewers**, a modern pub offering sport, beer and food on the Bulwark Road.

The only large modern hotel is on the Newport Road. It is now called the **Chepstow Hotel** but was the **Two Rivers** in the 1970s and the **Old Course** in the 1990s.

The landlord of the **Coach and Horses** was familiar with the following verse about some of the above pubs which were open between 1878 and 1882. The lines were composed at a later date:

> Joby James he kept the Pine Apple, Phil Penman kept the Dragon
> You had to have a pint or quart; they never stocked a flagon.
> Of course we had the Greyhound. A good old English dog,
> T'was close behind the Mitre, which was kept by Mrs Hogg.
> Dennis Driscoll kept the Queen's Head; Giles Griffiths Rose and Crown;
> Charles King was at the George Hotel before it was burnt down.
> Jack Benjamin the King's Head; William Price was at the Coach;
> Henry Phillips kept the Royal Oak, a house beyond reproach.

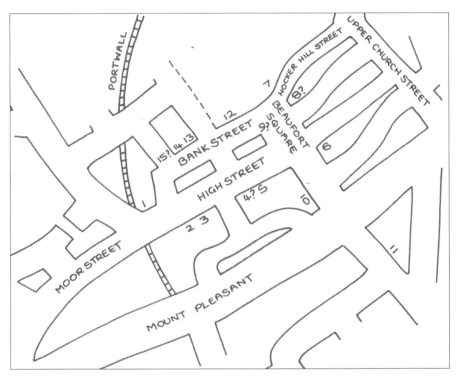

1.	**White Lion / Pye Corner**	9.	White Hart / Red Hart?
2.	Stone Kitchen	10.	Fountain
3.	Ship	11.	Berkeley
4.	Upper Crown?	12.	Wheatsheaf / Crown & Garter
5.	Bush	13.	Lamb & Flag
6.	**Beaufort Arms / Market House Inn**	14.	Bell Inn
		15.	Drum
7.	Three Cranes / Bath House		
8.	Crown & Anchor?		**Bold** open in 2007

CHEPSTOW – Chapter 12: High Street, Bank Street & Beaufort Square

CHAPTER TWELVE

Chepstow:
HIGH STREET, BANK STREET & BEAUFORT SQUARE

The walled town of Chepstow is accessed via the Town Gate, probably built in the 13th century at the same time as the Port Wall by Roger Bigod, although the present gate suggests a major rebuilding in the 15th or 16th centuries. The archway once had a gate where the market tolls were collected, and the room above has served as a guardroom, prison and museum. After the building was acquired by the Chepstow Council in 1899 another pedestrian entrance on the south side was constructed in 1928.

In 1905 Chepstow was 'one of those quaint and un-progressive country towns which have somehow managed to escape the effects of nineteenth century progress', but Keith Kissack in 1978 wrote:

the twentieth century has caught up with a vengeance. The centre of the town around the war memorial has recently been debased by an influx of the usual brand of cheap provincial supermarket architecture ... Chepstow's centre is dominated by the brutal black and white tower of Barclay's Bank ... The whole depressing area is flooded with traffic trying to get out. But although the centre once ringed by an almost continuous circuit of pubs has been sacrificed, the castle, the parish church, and even the station have been retained along with the bridges.

In 2005 the Chepstow High Street Regeneration Scheme was completed – a costly project that had been identified by the local councils, the chamber of commerce and the tourist office in 2001. They decided that the 'town was facing competition from neighbouring centres and thereby needed to start to build on its distinctive market town appeal'. The chosen artists worked closely with the design team and the local partnership so that the artwork 'reflected the town's culture and heritage as well as taking the town forward with some modern and contemporary influences'. The scheme included sculptures, poetry bands, stone columns, benches and walls all carved with appropriate themes.

The poetry bands depict lines from Welsh poets which are cleverly situated on the pavement outside suitable sites. There is 'Gateway to the town – goods prosperity and voices' by Menna Elfyn at the Town Gate with two lines written by the 18th-century poet, Rev. William Davies:

He who by land would enter Chepstow Town
Must quit his horse and lead him gently down.

An 1880s advertisement for the White Lion

And further lines from his Chepstow poem: 'In this snug town good meat and drink abound', on the pavement outside the wine merchant's shop.

Leading ahead from the Town Gate is the High Street which, according to the 1998 guide, 'has always been the main shopping street of the town and whilst a lot of the development of the recent past has removed much of the character that the street once had, interesting features remain'. On the left, one of the many stone plaques and arrows of the Chepstow Society's Heritage Trail is visible – the one in this corner informs that this was once known as Pye's Corner or White Lion Square, named after the inn sometimes known as the **House at Pye Corner**.

The **White Lion** sits comfortably in this corner

The White Lion plaque

with its large sign of a white lion and a neat plaque. In 1835, when William Marmont was the innkeeper, a coach called the *White Lion* carried passengers from Chepstow to Monmouth, Ross and Hereford, but was run by the **Beaufort Arms**. In 1837 Mary Hill was the landlady of this top of the town pub, but the **White Lion** was not recommended as an hotel, inn or posting house by Taylor in his *Guide* of 1860. During the 1870s and 1880s John Barrett kept the **White Lion** and opened his 'Wine and Spirit Vaults' with 'Ales and Spirits of the Finest Quality' and offered 'Beds & Private Sitting Rooms', and before the end of the 19th century was advertising 'Posting in all its Branches'.

The **White Lion** with its 'Large Panelled Bar, Living Room, Bagatelle Room, Kitchen, Pastrycook's Shop and Restaurant' together with four

An old photograph of the White Lion – it has changed little to the present day

A 1905 advertisement for the Bush Hotel

bedrooms, two attics, cellar, spacious yard, coach house, skittle alley and stabling for five horses was sold by the Duke of Beaufort in 1899. Up to this date the **White Lion's** address had been Back Street, but it was firmly placed by John Hill as 'White Lion hotel & dining rooms, High Street' in the 1901 directory, and in 1998 the **White Lion** was advertised as the 'Oldest Pub in

Ye Olde Bush Hotel

High Street, Chepstow

(Headquarters Cricket Club)
A.C.U. LISTED HOTEL.

———

LARGE OR SMALL PARTIES CATERED FOR.
GOOD ACCOMMODATION FOR TOURISTS.

Oldest Licensed House
—— in Chepstow. ——

———

Centre of Town.   Garage on Premises.
Billiards.   Telephone 259.

———

Proprietor :   GEORGE H. HUTCHINGS

The 1925 advertisement was not as attractive as the earlier one

Chepstow' with 'New Menus' in Bank Street, and was still open in 2006.

Walking from the Town Gate to Beaufort Square it is noted from the Chepstow Society's informative plaques that 8 High Street, on the right-hand side, was at one time a licensed premises called the **Stone Kitchen**. The last known landlord of this unusually-named pub was Edmund Davis in 1831. Further down and understood to be on the same side of High Street was the **Ship Alehouse,** recorded in 1815 as having been 'used for many years as a private dwelling house, now occupied by John Reynolds adjoining a skinners yard'. There was also the **Upper Crown** in 1716 leased for one year from Richard Jones to William Badam and the **Three Crowns** auctiond in 1800.

The most remembered pub on this side of the street was the **Bush**, established in the 1850s by the Davies family who appear to have previously run a wine and spirit merchants in the same property – a medieval building with a Georgian façade. The plaque outside the site of the **Bush** relates that a spiral staircase wound around a single tree trunk runs from the cellar to the attic within a stair turret, and that there was a medieval window in the cellar. The Davies remained at the **Bush** into the 1870s, and by 1905 it was named **Ye Olde Bush Hotel** with an unfounded claim to have been 'The Oldest-established House in the Town'. The proprietor W.G. Oliver served 'Luncheons, Dinners, Teas, Wines and Spirits of Best Quality' and offered 'Good Accommodation for Cyclists'.

Ye Olde Bush Hotel was kept by George Hutchings in 1925 and by Richard Radaelli in 1937. Having survived the Second World War, the **Bush Hotel** hit the headlines of the *South Wales Argus* in 1963 when it was reported that the 'Bush Hotel Chepstow Site will now be redeveloped'. The paper continued that the 'site which had been valued at £45,000, is not to be preserved as a building of architectural and historical interest', although the council had turned down Messrs. Truman's application to redevelop the site, the Minister of Housing allowed the old building to be demolished. Other pubs in the High Street were the **Greyhound** of 1822 and two listed by Ivor Waters – the **Crown** and the **Lower Crown**.

Beaufort Square in 1885

Beaufort Square is the heart of Chepstow – an open space where fairs and markets were once held, but remodelled around the war memorial of 1921 and overlooked by the oversized bank building of 1970 and redesigned once again by the Regeneration Scheme in 2005. The market traders, business men and visitors of the past would have been attracted to this area where at least two inns were open in the mid-18th century and another is known to have been open in the early 1800s. Pevsner describes the 'Beaufort Arms, with a three-storeyed front of five bays plus with an off-centre entrance attached to its r[ight], the stuccoed Assembly Rooms of 1807'. A document of 1760 records this inn as the **Beaufort Arms** or **Market House Inn** and in 1813 it is mentioned in a lease as **Market House** or **Beaufort Arms Inn**

The **Beaufort** was a popular meeting place where a coffee room was planned in 1814 to be in the 'upper front Parlour of the Beaufort's Arms Inn, and be entirely appropriated to the Use of the Subscribers as a Coffee Room, except for Travellers, who will at all Times be at liberty to occupy the Room'. Newspapers, reviews, books and maps were to be made available to the subscribers who paid 'One Guinea per Annum' to the treasurer Mr. John Evans. Apart from serving refreshments and offering accommodation the inn had other functions such as holding auction sales and meetings of the

Monmouthshire and Gloucestershire.

SUPERIOR

Navy, Plank Logs,

AND OTHER

TIMBER.

To be Sold by Auction,

BY R. WHITE AND SON,

At the Beaufort Arms Inn, Chepstow,

On SATURDAY, the 31st Day of March, 1821,

At FOUR o'Clock in the Afternoon,

(SUBJECT TO CONDITIONS OF SALE TO BE THEN PRODUCED;)

THE FOLLOWING LOTS

OF

OAK TIMBER,

Which are well calculated for Navy Thickstuff, Plank & Frame Timber.

Lots 1, 2, 3, 4, 5, 6, and 7, are growing upon Bigswear Estate, adjoining the River Wye, about 7 Miles from the Port of Chepstow; and Lots 8 and 9, are growing upon Ifton Estate, which is distant about 7 Miles from the said Port of Chepstow, (to which it communicates by a very good Road,) and about 2 Miles from the Severn at Caldicot Pill.

LOT I.

120 OAK TREES, numbered with White Paint, growing in the *Hill Grounds* and *Great Orchard*, Bigswear.

LOT II.

300 Capital OAK TREES, of great Length, numbered with White Paint, growing in the *Lower Tufts Grove.*

LOT III.

200 Capital OAK TREES, numbered with White Paint, growing in *Red-Hill* and *Upper Tufts Grove, Widow's Field, Red-Hill, and Long Meadows.*

LOT IV.

140 ASH TREES, numbered with White Paint, growing in the *Hill Grounds, Tuft Woods, and Lands adjoining.*

LOT V.

11 ELM TREES, and 1 SYCAMORE TREE, numbered with White Paint, growing in a Meadow at *Landogo,* adjoining the River Wye.

LOT VI.

20 OAK TREES numbered with White Paint, growing upon Lands in *Hewelsfield,* in the Occupation of Mr. Thomas Hughes.

LOT VII.

79 ASH TREES and 1 WALNUT TREE, numbered with White Paint. growing upon Lands in *Hewelsfield* aforesaid.

LOT VIII.

300 OAK TREES, numbered with White Paint, growing on *Ifton Estate.*

LOT IX.

20 *ELM TREES,* ditto   ditto.

For a View of the Lots at Bigswear, apply to Mr. WM. MATTHEWS, Woodward, at the Florence, near St. Briavells; and those at Ifton, to the Tenant; and for further Particulars to the Auctioneers, at Coleford, or to MR. JAMES EVANS, Solicitor, Chepstow.

MAJOR, Printer, Chepstow.

A sale of timber at the Beaufort Arms Inn in 1821.

CHEPSTOW . . .

Beaufort Arms Hotel.

Old=established First=class Hotel for Families and Gentlemen.

SANITARY ARRANGEMENTS ARE OF THE LATEST APPROVED SYSTEM.

Near the Histronic Castle, founded in the 11th century, and surrounded by Scenery of the Loveliest description.

Tintern Abbey and the Wye Valley.

OMNIBUS TO MEET ALL TRAINS.

POSTING.

Telephone No. 0197 (National).

For Terms apply to MISS PROBERT, Manageress.

106

Beaufort Arms advertisement in 1905 included the Market Hall and the Assembly Rooms

The Beaufort had changed its image by 1965

Turnpike Trustees, the Farmers' Club, the Chepstow County Club, and providing an office for the Chepstow Steeplechasers.

From 1871 the adjoining Market House was incorporated into the hotel with an assembly room above which balls and concerts were held. In 1899 the **Beaufort Arms** was for sale as: 'The Important and Well Established Freehold Fully-Licensed Property' with its commercial room, smoke room, double-fronted bar, offices, still room and pantry. On the opposite side of the covered carriage way was the County Club room, the Market Room and the night porter's bedroom. There was also 23 bedrooms, a large ball and concert room and extensive cellars. At the rear was the servant's hall, a billiard room, an ostler's cottage and numerous stables and two coach houses.

The Beaufort Arms in 2000

The manageress of the **Beaufort Arms** in 1905 was Miss Probert, who was running a hotel that had sanitary arrangements, a telephone, and an omnibus to meet the trains. And by 1925 the new resident proprietors were advertising modern conveniences and garaging. During the 1920s the **Beaufort Arms Hotel** had been acquired by Beauchamp Bros. and Williams and by 1950 it was a John Watts Hotel, approved by the AA and RAC. More recently the hotel has become privately owned, being described as being in the 'Heart of Chepstow'.

On the opposite side of Beaufort Square is a handsome house called St. Maur, which was the **Three Cranes Inn** with an interesting history dating from 1697. During the early 18th century John Morgan kept the inn, which later that century was visited by the

The Nelson plaque

Hon. John Byng while touring Chepstow in 1781. Byng stayed at the **Three Cranes**, and wrote in his *Torrington Diaries*:

> The Cranes Inn (where I stopp'd) and the Beaufort Arms Inn, being both hired by the same person, brings on a certain imposition, from which the traveller cannot fly. ... At the door [of the Three Cranes] was a bevy of Welsh squires intoxicating themselves; and round the market-place, plenty of puppet-shews, balance masters, etc.etc. but the heat of the weather prevented my going to see them.

A decade later a lease refers to the inn known by the sign of the **Bath House** or **Three Cranes**, but it was the latter name that remained in use.

During Nelson's tour of South Wales in 1802, he and his companions stayed at the **Three Cranes**, an event that is now commemorated on a bronze plaque. According to Edward Gill in *Nelson and the Hamiltons on Tour* published in 1987, an amusing incident occurred concerning a sailor, whom Nelson eventually recognised by the way he drank his soup, so the admiral gave him a few shillings. As no further documentation has been found after this date, it is assumed that the inn closed and the building was renamed St. Maur.

St. Maur – once the Three Cranes

The other pubs known to have been in the Square were the **Crown and Anchor**, kept by Hannah Smart in 1835 and possibly up to 1858 when the property was not re-licensed, and the **White Hart**, which was probably the **Red Hart** of 1697 becoming the **White Hart** by 1795. James Roach was there in 1835 and was followed by George Ward. This was between 1842 and 1852 when a friendly society held their meetings at the inn. In 1858 the license was transferred from James Dobbs to Ann Dobbs and an Elizabeth Dobbs was listed at the inn during the 1870s. The Bicycle Club had their headquarters at the **White Hart** about the time it became a Temperance Hotel.

The drunks 'intoxicating themselves' observed by Byng in 1781 was a continual occurrence that was regularly reported in the *Chepstow Weekly Advertiser* and the *Monmouth Beacon* during the 19th century. In 1888 'James Higgins and Charles Richards were charged with being drunk and riotous at Chepstow on the 25th March – Higgins was fined 5s. and 5s. costs, and Richards 2s. 6d. fine and 5s. costs', whilst in the same report Samuel Richards and William Swaine were ordered by Petty Sessions to pay costs for 'committing a breach of the peace by fighting at Chepstow' most likely to have been caused by heavy drinking. In 1897 Thomas Holmer, a tailor, was charged with being drunk and indecent, and Mary Lewis, a stranger, was charged for drunkenness and using filthy language. In 1898 at the Chepstow Police Court, 'John Gill, a tramp, was charged for being drunk and riotous at Chepstow ... he used most disgusting language and was very riotous and very drunk', but only fined 2s. 6d. and costs.

From Beaufort Square, Station Road led in an easterly direction from the centre of the old town, but this road has now become detached and partly obscured by the construction of the inner relief road in 1988. The station was built for the South Wales Railway as Bradney in 1904 wrote:

> The railway from Gloucester to Chepstow and on to Newport and Cardiff was commenced about the year 1847. It was opened for traffic by 1850, but, the bridges not being ready, passengers were conveyed by road from Chepstow station to a temporary station at Snipe's Hill in Tidenham. By 1852 the bridge was finished and the line completed.

The Wye Valley line to Monmouth was opened in 1876 making Chepstow a busy station with two nearby pubs. Along Station Road was the **Fountain Hotel** on the corner of Upper Nelson Street. John Perkins was the landlord in 1835 followed by Benjamin Sargent before the license was transferred to William Marin in 1858. It became a Stroud Brewery house and in 1962 the 'Inn in Nelson Street Chepstow known as the Fountain Inn with the outbuildings and land thereto adjoining and belonging' was taken over by

Ready for an outing at the Fountain Hotel

A 1965 advertisement

The one time Berkeley Arms

West Country Breweries. The Corbins were at the **Fountain** in 1965 serving simple food before it finally closed and was demolished in 1972

Another pub in Station Road, also near the car park, was known as the **Berkeley Arms** in 1962 when it passed from the Stroud Brewery to West Country Breweries. Alf Hughes was the tenant serving 'West Country Beers' in 1970 and was succeeded by Mrs. Morton when closure was threatened in 1983. The *South Wales Argus* reported that the **Berkeley** was to be sold by Whitbread (who had taken over West Country Breweries) at an asking price of £50,000 as 'part of the company's rationalisation plan and a question of maintenance ... barrelage has fallen over the last three years and the amount of money taken does not make it economically viable to continue'. Mrs. Morton had been there for eleven years and regretted leaving, but she and her husband were not prepared to pay over £49,000 for the pub. Also in Station Street was the one time **Prince of Wales** listed by Waters.

From Beaufort Square there is another street called Bank Street that runs parallel to High Street back towards the Town Gate. In Bank Street there was once a row of inns and the remaining documentation does not make it easy to distinguish one from another. From the corner of Beaufort Square there was the **Wheatsheaf**, which was known as the **Crown and Garter** in 1733, and originally stood on the existing derelict site in Bank Street. The assignment of mortgage of 1831 records a:

> messuage etc. with yard and brewhouse together with three rooms upstairs under the roof of the adjoining dwelling house, also all that cellar under the shop formerly part of the adjoining [and] altogether called the Crown and Garter lying near a place called the Square now commonly called the Wheatsheaf bounded by the White Hart and the Lamb and Flag.

In 1835 Rachael Morgan's family at the **Wheatsheaf** appear to have served as the last licensees.

The **Lamb and Flag** was recorded in a mortgage of 1814:

> All that messuage, tenement or dwelling house (whereto a Smith's Forge formerly belonged) called the Lamb and Flag with the garden, stable, outhouses and premises thereto belonging in the tenure of Roger Williams or his undertenants afterwards of William Hodges and now of the said Lewis Price.

Once the Lamb and Flag

Long since closed as an inn, the building still stands, and according to Pevsner 'the stone end wall of No. 13, corbelled out at mid-height, may have belonged to a 16th-century timber-framed front with a jetty'. It stands next door to the old **Bell** which has been converted into shops and flats, but still displays a sign 'Old Bell Chambers' outside its rather severe 18th-century front.

The **Bell** in 1814 was 'late in the tenure of Ann Whitford but now of Geo Brooke', and during the 1830s and '40s was kept by Thomas Ivins. William Holland took over in the

The Bell in 1963

1850s when the **Bell** was used as a court house and a place where weights and measures were checked by a visiting inspector. From 1871, when Jane Griffiths was the tenant, there is a lack of documentation, but by 1937 John Phillips was at the **Bell** when the premises were acquired by Arnold Perrett and Co. as:

> All that messuage tenement dwellinghouse and Inn with the garden yard stable store rooms and outbuildings thereto adjoining and belonging situate lying and being in Bank Street in the Town of Chepstow in the County of Monmouth and called or known by the sign of the Bell Hotel.

Probably one of the last advertisements for the **Bell** appeared in 1965, before it closed in 1972, when the proprietors were Mr. and Mrs. Flowers running a 'Fully Licensed' residential hotel.

In Taylor's *Guide to the banks of the Wye*, the **Bell** was included in his list written in the 1860s:

> Chepstow is an improving town, possessing many handsome shops, is well lighted, and has excellent accommodation for visitors, at the hotels, inns and lodging-house. The Hotels are – The Beaufort Arms and George, both of which are posting houses. The Inns are – The White Hart – The Bell – The Horn – The Bridge Inn – The Greyhound – The King's Head – and the Green Dragon.

The Bell and the one-time Drum

The last known pub in this line of inns was the **Drum**, which had already closed by 1814 when a deed records that 'the premises were [previously] occupied by Michael Morgan deceased, but now of James Morgan formerly known by the name of the Drum'. The **Drum** is an unusual inn sign – in other places there have been Drummer and Drum Major, both signs normally associated with the military, and also the Drum and Monkey probably referring to the travelling showmen who once toured the country with a monkey that performed tricks on a drum.

The verse below is understood to have been written in the 1870s, but Charlie Dobbs was not at the **Bell** until the 1890s, so it must have been written at a later date:

> And just below the Town Gate, a pub you could rely on,
> Twas kept by William Barrett; you remember the White Lion?
> Miss Stobart kept the Bush, I knew the lady well,
> And Charlie Dobbs would always bid you welcome at the Bell.
> And here we see the Beaufort Arms, it stands in Beaufort-square,
> Mrs Garrett is the lady that reigns supremely there;
> It's quite a fashionable hotel, and one can plainly see
> Its patronage is found amongst the aristocracy.

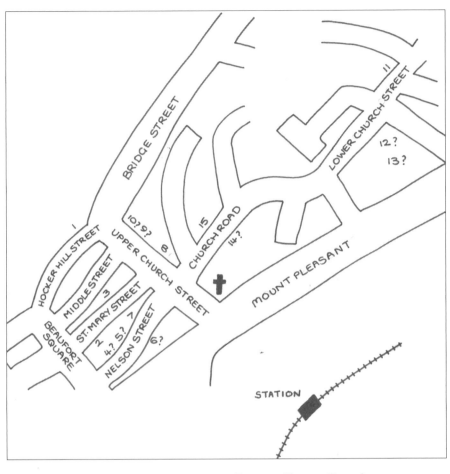

1.	**Five Alls**	7.	**Jimmy Dean's**
2.	Rummer / Vaults	8.	Plough
3.	**The Grape / Grape Escape**	9.	King's Arms?
		10.	Bunch of Grapes?
4.	Freemason's Arms / Masons / Jolly Sailor?	11.	Three Salmons
		12.	Butcher's Arms?
		13.	Victoria?
5.	Brewer's Arms?	14.	Golden Heart?
6.	Nelson Arms?	15.	Railway Tavern

CHAPTER 13 – Chepstow: Hocker Hill, St. Mary's, Nelson and the Church Streets

CHAPTER THIRTEEN

Chepstow:
HOCKER HILL, ST. MARY'S, NELSON & THE CHURCH STREETS

From Beaufort Square – the heart of Chepstow, which once formed the market place – a parallel line of narrow streets called Hocker Hill, Middle, St. Mary's and Nelson Streets join into Upper Church Street. It is understood that the early Norman settlement of Chepstow probably grew along the line of Upper Church Street between the priory and the castle. It appears from earlier maps, plans and records of the town that several street names have changed, although the pattern of streets remains little altered since the end of the 18th century. In 1801 Upper Church Street was known as St. Mary's Street, Nelson Street was shown as Back Lane (which possibly follows the line of a Roman route) and, according to the *Chepstow Heritage Trail* plaque, Church Road was called Horse Lane. The most significant change to the streets of Chepstow was the construction of the inner relief road which carries the main A48 road south of the church to the new bridge built over the river Wye in 1988.

In 1905 a visitor arriving at the station would not have been favourably impressed – 'the streets are narrow, and many of the houses antiquated, and even squalid. There are however many picturesque bits of architecture' and this early 20th century *Wye Valley Guide* continued to record that a few years ago:

> a visit to St. Mary's Parish Church was a very depressing task to the lover of ancient architecture ... Now, however a judicious restoration has stripped the old work of its casing of stucco and whitewash and disfiguring galleries, with the result that the nave with its unique triforium is now both handsome and interesting.

The church is sober but impressive with monuments inside and in the churchyard commemorating past merchants and vintners of the town.

The priory buildings and the present parish church of St. Mary were built around 1072 on land given by William fitz Osbern, Lord of Chepstow, a town then know as Stiguil. As a Benedictine monastery, the nave of the priory church was also used by the townsfolk, and after the Dissolution the property, apart from the nave of the church, was ordered to be demolished. Thus, when Leyland visited Chepstow a few years later, he noted that the town had one parish church and that the 'celle of a Blake Monk or two of Bermondsey by London was lately there suppressed'. By the early 17th century the greater part of the priory had been demolished apart from the parish church. Archaeological evidence suggests that the 12th-century western range had been demolished at an earlier period, and that a new range had been built that included a cellar, which was later used as a bonded wine store. This is a securely locked store or cellar where liquor is kept under Customs control until duty or excise has been paid. Other surviving buildings associated with the priory continued to be used as a brewery and a creamery until 1965.

In the 1820s Charles Heath recorded that the church 'is situated in the lower part of the town, – a few hundred yards to the eastward of the Castle, – and from being nearly surrounded by orcharding and fruit trees, it exhibits, in the blossom season, the most beautiful and picturesque appearance'. This description is confirmed on the 1801 map showing fields and orchards surrounding the church. This pleasant-sounding scene has since been lost forever and the whole area replaced by the busy and noisy A48 road, its adjacent car parks, subway, unsightly road signs and a supermarket.

The castle, lying at the western end of Upper Church street, has faired better on its magnificent cliff top situation overlooking the Wye, which

Chepstow Castle guards the mouth of the Wye

Pevsner describes as 'one of the exhilarating and instructive castles in the whole of Britain'. In the recently published *Chepstow Castle: its History and Buildings* it is described as:

> one of the most remarkable castles in Britain. From the outside, the history of fortification can be traced from the Norman Conquest to the end of the 17th century. On the inside, there are suites of accommodation intended for both ceremonial and domestic use., built and adapted for some of the greatest men of the Middle Ages and Tudor periods.

There was no need for a brew house in the castle, because the earl had a *prise* – a proportionary tax of all the ale brewed in the borough – which could have been commuted for cash if there was no demand for the beer. The ale would have been delivered by boat and hoisted into the cellar from the quay. During the Welsh war it was recorded that 18 barrels and 6 measures of ale worth 12s. together with quantities of meat, bread, fish and poultry were consumed in the castle between 28 January and 8 February 1285.

From Beaufort Square, Hocker Hill Street (known as Hawker Street in 1835 when Ann Phillips was recorded as a beer retailer) leads down a picturesque cobbled lane where, in 2007, the **Five Alls** was advertised as:

> A pub since 1847, situated at the bottom of the only cobbled street left in Chepstow. Renowned for its Rock, Juke Box and live music. A cosy atmospheric pub, popular amongst young and old alike. Home to Hobgoblin cask ales such as Speckled Hen, Otters, Tribute and many more.

Earlier publicans include Thomas Barge in 1871, Elizabeth Richards in 1901, William Bevan in 1937 and Ben Brown in the 1960s when the **Five**

The Five Alls in 2006

Alls was 'The only Courage House in Town' serving 'EIPA and AK'. The former refers to East India Pale Ale but the latter is unknown to the author.

The colourful sign of the **Five Alls** depicts a soldier 'I fight for all'; a parson 'I pray for all'; a king 'I rule all'; a lawyer 'I plead for all'; and John Bull 'I pay for all'. This type of sign dates from the 17th century in the West Country, and some show a labourer instead of John Bull, others show six 'alls' which includes the Devil 'I Take All', while the sign for four 'alls' refers to:

> King William thinks all
> Queen Mary takes all
> Prince George drinks all
> Princess Anne eats all

Almost adjoining the **Five Alls** are the Powis's Almshouses built in 1721 under the terms of Thomas Powis's will. In the 1820s Charles Heath recorded the weathered inscription:

This Alms House was erected and endowed, anno Domini 1716, by the sole charity of Thomas Powis, late of Enfield, in the county of Middlesex, Vintner, a native of the town, for the reception and maintenance of six poor men and six poor women, inhabitants of this parish, for ever.

Heath knew little of the founder, but assumed he left Chepstow as a young man and successfully traded as a wine merchant.

The Heritage Trail plaque adds the information that the cellar below the almshouses was used as a wine store by Richard Fydell in the late 18th century as immortalised by Chepstow's poet Edward Davies in 1784:

Beneath one house a spacious cellar stands
Well scor'd with wine but in a Vintners hands
And although old George cannot command a flask
He, like Diogenes, may smell the Cask.

Middle Street and St. Mary's Street run parallel to Hocker Hill Street from Beaufort Square, but the rather dreary Middle Street does not appear to have any known pubs; only a beer retailer in the mid-19th century. On the south side of St. Mary's Street, which was pedestrianised in 1991, was the **Rummer**, leased from Esther Baldwyn, widow, to James Davis in 1824 as 'All that messuage, tenement or dwelling house formerly used as a public house and commonly called or known by the name of the Rummer with its outbuildings, courtyards and appurtenances'. In 1858 the licensee was James Davis, who named it the **Vaults** in 1859, but in 1871 Richard Hawkesford was the landlord when it was once again the **Rummer**. The **Vaults** sign indicates that the premises were used to store wine and other liquors, and is frequently added to other names. According to Dunkling and Wright the **Rummer** sign has nothing to do with rum; it is a large drinking glass, the word deriving from the Flemish or Dutch *roemer*. It is traditionally explained as meaning 'Roman' glass. However, according to Andre Simon it dates from the late-18th century and takes its name from a large heavy glass called a rummer, from rum, 'the

A 'rummer' glass

217

basis of all good Punch, that most convivial and popular hot drink of the period'. He states that the heavy Rummer glasses were used for both Punch and Grog, the difference between them being that Punch was mixed in company and consumed among friends, whereas Grog was mixed and consumed individually.

The one-time Rummer

The Flowers and Harvey families were long serving publicans at the **Rummer** during the first half of the 20th century when it was acquired by Arnold Perrett & Co. before it was taken over by Cheltenham Original Brewery in 1937 as:

> All That messuage or tenement with yard attached and appurtenances thereto situate on the south side of St Mary Street Chepstow in the County of Monmouth and having a messuage and premises lately of Emma Garrett on the ease and a messuage and premises lately of Thomas Harris on the west and the messuages secondly hereinafter described at the back or south thereof which said messuage land and herediments are used as an Inn or Public House known by the name or sign of The Rummer Inn.

The conveyance also records a stable and yard on the south side, 'formerly four cottages situate in Benson's Court', and 'All That dwelling-house being formerly two cottages or tenements known as Numbers 27 and 28 Nelson Street'. Some time after this take-over the **Rummer** closed.

Almost opposite is the **Grape Food and Wine Bar**, a recently licensed premises in St. Mary Street. It was called the **Grape Escape** in 1998, offering bar meals all day, an 'A La Carte Restaurant', and morning coffee and after-noon teas in a relaxed and unique atmosphere.

Unfortunately from January 2007 the **Grape** has had competition for good coffee and tea at 'Coffee 1', which opened next to the **Beaufort Arms**

The Grape Food and Wine Bar in 2006

in what had once been part of the inn. There was also a pub called the **Moon**, researched by Waters in St. Mary Street.

Nelson Street is the fourth parallel street from Beaufort Square, but it is the one that has suffered the most dramatic changes. Car parks and the A48 road dominate this once rather narrow back lane, and much redevelopment has taken place. Even in 1898 property including shops, dwelling houses, tenements, warehouses, stables and a carpenter's shop were for sale between Nelson Street and St. Mary Street. They were occupied by James Creese, whose family had been brewers in 1859, and licensees of the **Freemason's Arms** in Nelson Street during the 1850s.

This inn was also known as the **Jolly Sailor** and was recorded simply as the **Mason's** in 1830 before Frances Williams took over in 1849. Arnold Perrett & Co. purchased the premises in 1900 from Thirza Williams who continued as the landlady into 1901. Allen Dibden was the publican in 1937 when the Cheltenham Original Brewery took over:

> All That messuage or dwellinghouse now and for many years past used as a fully licensed Inn formerly called or known by the name of the Jolly Sailor but now the Freemason's Arms and all outbuildings and appurtenances thereto belonging situate in Nelson Street.

Since then the pub has closed and the site has been redeveloped. Also in Nelson Street was a **Brewer's Arms** kept by Mary Kitchen in 1862 which may have been yet another name for the **Freemason's**.

Surprisingly, the **Nelson Arms** was actually in Nelson Street and dated from at least 1825 when a lease recorded the pub was 'called or known by the name or sign of the Nelson Arms in Nelson Street since in tenure to Thomas Thomas and now occupied by Giles Griffiths'. Robert Burges, William

Hopkins and Rachael Ridgeway held the license before 1858. Several others followed including Dorcas Waters who appears to have served as the last publican before the inn closed in the early 20th century. There was also a beer retailer in Nelson Street belonging to Morgan Jones in 1849 and another run by John Lewis in 1859. In addition there was the **Paul Pry** as listed by Waters. The name may well have been taken from a barge which transported goods along the river Wye from Hereford, but according to Dunkling and White in their book *Pub Names of Britain* it is more likely to refer to a play by John Poole produced in 1828 with the title character being a man who constantly meddles in other people's affairs because he has nothing to do himself. The play was popular and signs often appeared in a town after its performance at the local theatre. Inn signs show Paul Pry listening at doors marked 'private' etc.

The only licensed establishment in Nelson Street is a nightclub called **Jimmy Dean**, which appears to have a rather notorious reputation. Since its establishment in the 21st century there was an incident in 2003 reported by *BBC Wales* regarding 'a former Miss Wales being cleared of attacking a woman with a broken bottle in a row with a lap dancer over who was the prettiest'. In 2006 Gwent police were appealing for information about an assault that occurred in **Jimmy Deans Public House** when a male received serious facial injuries and was taken to hospital.

Nelson Street leads to St. Mary's church and Upper Church Street where a few inns have been identified including the **Plough**, kept by Elisha Williams in 1862 and by Samuel Price in 1871. This was a beer house which finally closed its doors in 1939. There was also the **King's Arms** at number four which existed well into the 1960s, its owners, the Stroud Brewery, being sold to West Country Breweries in 1962. The **King's Arms** was an early 19th-century inn kept by William Bradshaw in 1835, Richard Hawkesford in 1849 (before he went to the **Rummer**), and David Dorwood in 1859. Henry Hemmens sold the premises in 1889 to the Stroud Brewery and in 1937 Ernest Price was listed as a beer retailer at the same address. Other inns were the **Hope and Anchor** of 1859 kept by

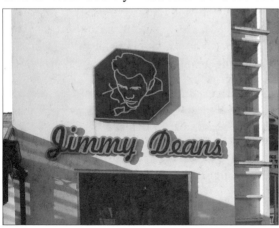

Jimmy Dean's

220

Matthew Baker and the **Bunch of Grapes,** licensed by William Phelps in 1858, William Hooper in 1901 and John Delaney in 1937.

Church Road curves around St. Mary's churchyard and continues as Lower Church Street. Leading off these streets are some attractive courtyards and rows of cottages including Church Row, Howells Row, Hollins Close and Kendal Square, which were described in the 1998 *Chepstow Town Guide* as demonstrating 'a close harmony between old and new architecture'. Amongst the houses and cottages in Church Road and Lower Church Street were at least seven licensed premises in the mid-19th century – five were named pubs and two were unnamed beer-houses. Behind the houses near the Drill Hall were apple orchards and hop gardens, which may well have provided the necessary ingredients for cider and beer making in the 18th century.

The oldest known pub along Church Road and Church Street was the **Three Salmons**, recorded in deeds of 1796 and 1833 as a 'Messuage called Three Salmons Public House ... bounded by the Highway leading from Chepstow Churchyard'. From the 1830s to its closure around 1871 the Woodgate family kept the inn together with a grocers shop and a builder's yard in Lower Church Street. The **Butcher's Arms** in the same street had been established by the early 19th century and was run consecutively by John Hatton, William Willetts and William Twining before it closed around 1860 when the **Victoria**, kept by Elizabeth Lewes, opened for a short period.

In Church Road there was the **Golden Heart** of 1849 kept by Mary Cole, whilst the later **Railway Tavern** was opened by Leonard Probert in the early 1850s to cater for passengers travelling on the South Wales Line. The Proberts continued to run the **Railway** until around 1880 when a succession of different landlords took over including William Henderson in 1901 and Albert Smith in 1937 who was recorded as the last landlord.

In the past there were several other inns and beer houses in Upper and Lower Church Streets as recorded by Ivor Waters. They include the **Antelope**, the **Bull**, the **Lamb**, the **Ship** and the **Bob Inn**.

The rhyme about *Chepstow Inns and Taverns* written around 1920 includes for this chapter:

> Another cosy place in winter or in summer,
> A fine old English gentleman was Roberts of the Rummer.
> Fred Smith was at the King's Arms, Bill Hooper kept the Bunch;
> You could always get a double there or a fine bowl of punch.
> William Barge was at the Five Alls, John Ely at the Plough,
> That's over fifty years ago, wherever are they now?

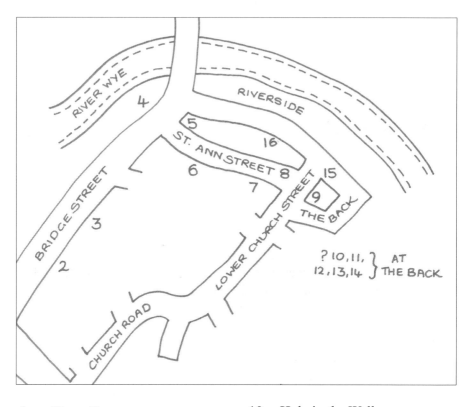

1.	**Three Tuns**	10.	Hole in the Wall
2.	**Chepstow Castle**	11.	Prince Regent
3.	**Castle View**	12.	New Zealand
4.	**Afon Gwy / Full Moon**	13.	Cooper's Arms
5.	**Bridge**	14.	Steam Packet
6.	Lord Wellington	15.	**Chepstow Boat / Boat**
7.	Sailor's Tavern/Old England	16.	**Salutation / Lord Russell /**
8.	Wye House		**Wye Knot / Petrus**
9.	Mermaid/Lord Nelson	**Bold** open in 2007	

CHEPSTOW – Chapter 14: Bridge Street, St. Ann Street and The Back

CHAPTER FOURTEEN

Chepstow:
BRIDGE STREET, ST. ANN STREET & THE BACK

Bridge Street, with its elegant row of early 19th-century houses, descends to the Wye which is crossed by a graceful cast-iron bridge of 1816 designed by John Rennie. This links Welsh Monmouthshire to English Gloucestershire and carries present day motorists and walkers onto the Offa's Dyke Walk, the Gloucestershire Way and to the many pubs described in the companion volume – *The Pubs of the Royal Forest of Dean*. The iron bridge replaced an earlier timber one which, according to Heath, was 'curiously constructed, in consequence of the High Tides peculiar to this part of the river, which flow more than Forty feet above the bed of it at low water, and have been known as high as Fifty'. On the Gloucestershire side of the Wye the old turnpike road led straight up the hill along the present day footpath, before being re-routed in 1808 around Castleford Hill to provide an easier gradient for horse-drawn vehicles.

Of all the streets in Chepstow, Bridge Street has faired the best for the survival of pubs and hotels. It is the street that attracts visitors and tourists for there is a large car and coach park with an adjoining Tourist Information Centre. It also includes the entrance to Chepstow Castle, which is opposite the Museum, and there is easy access to the bridge and the attractive riverside gardens. From the top of Bridge Street the first noticeable pub is the **Three Tuns** which was already established by 1829 when John Brown, victualler, leased:

> All that messuage tenement or dwelling house with the garden, brewhouse, stable, outhouses, buildings, yards and premises occupied by John Brown and commonly called or known by the sign of the Three Tuns ... bounded by Bridge Street, a certain pool called the Castle Ditch Pool and the roadway leading from Bridge Street to Chepstow Castle.

John Brown continued as the victualler at the **Three Tuns** throughout the 1830s before other publicans including Thomas Jones, Edward Bevan, Eliza Jones and Mary Richards took over. While Mary Richards was the landlady in 1899, the 'Freehold and Tithe Free Public House known as the Three Tuns' was offered for sale alongwith several other Duke of Beaufort's pubs and inns. The **Three Tuns** was 'entered by a broad stone-flagged passage' and contained 'Living Room, Parlour, Large Bar, Back Kitchen and Loft Over, also Spacious Cellar'. On the first floor there were three bedrooms, and the pub adjoined a cottage, stabling, a trap house and a yard with 'a gate opening on to the Castle Entrance'. A tun is a large cask for wines and other liquids with a capacity of two pipes or four hogsheads or 282 old wine gallons. Three tuns appear on the arms of the Worshipful Company of Vintners as well as the Worshipful Company of Brewers, hence the widespread use of this sign.

CHEPSTOW.—THE THREE TUNS.

ALL THAT messuage or Public House known as The Three Tuns situate at Number 31 Bridge Street in the Town of Chepstow in the County of Monmouth TOGETHER with the cottage and yard adjoining thereto and all outbuildings and appurtenances thereunto belonging TOGETHER with the sites thereof and the land occupied therewith respectively.

The 1937 sale of the Three Tuns to the Cheltenham Original Brewery

The Three Tuns in 2006

*The Three Tuns became
Porter's Ale House*

During the 20th century Arnold Perrett and Co. acquired the inn and in 1937, while William Lewis was the tenant, it passed to the Cheltenham Original Brewery and later became a Whitbread House as can be seen from the sign shown on photographs since 1963. In 1998 the **Three Tuns** was known as **Porter's Ale House**. It is still thriving in 2007.

On the opposite side of Bridge Street is the **Chepstow Castle** bearing a Courage sign, serving Guest Ales and meals. It was in 1975 that 'Chepstow' was added to the previous simple **Castle**, which is understood to occupy the same site as the **Hotel de Chile** of 1871 kept by Benjamin Evans.

A little further along is the attractive looking **Castle View Hotel**, which the owners claim:

Chepstow Castle Inn, 2006

was built about 300 years ago as a private residence originally called Westfield House. The first owner was the local factory owner. It is interesting to think that its stones may have come from Chepstow Castle, just across the road, which by that time had fallen into disuse. The solid walls and foundations of the original building are up to five feet thick, tapering to a mere three feet to carry the seasoned oak roof supports.

CASTLE VIEW HOTEL
A.A. & R.A.C. Recommended

Props.: Mervyn & Lucia Gillett

"Our aim is to provide comfort, good food and personal attention in surroundings which retain the charm of the eighteenth century."

Tel.: CHEPSTOW 3565

Facing Castle and Car Park

Castle View, 1975

The **Castle View** opened as a hotel in 1950 and in 1990 the local press reported that due to a 'boom in mini holidays' outline planning permission was 'being sought for eleven extra bedrooms at the Castle View Hotel which is run by Martin Cardale and his wife Vicky'. In 1998 meals were available from the 'Commended restaurant and bar' in an hotel that aimed to 'provide good food and a friendly welcome in surroundings which retain the charm of the 18th century'. In 2006 Wye Valley brews were available.

Near the bottom of Bridge Street is a grade II listed building now called **Afon Gwy**. It was built in 1735 and from at least 1830 served as the **Full Moon** licensed to Mary Gwatkin until the 1870s. Others

Castle View Hotel in 2006

226

Afon Gwy – River Wye – *in 2006*

followed and Charles Fox in 1901 probably served as one of the last land-lords at this inn on the Wye. The occupiers in 2006 purchased the premises in 1986 and renamed it **Afon Gwy** (the Welsh for River Wye) and opened the old pub as a restaurant with a lounge bar.

The **Full Moon** is a convenient visual inn sign, and sometimes shortened to the **Moon** or changed to the **Half Moon**. One sign was known to display:

> Step in my friends, and take a cup;
> It is not dark, for the moon is up.
> Sit down refresh, and pay your way,
> Then you will call another day.

Before reaching the Wye, the **Bridge Inn**, on the east side of the road, has remained open since its origins in the 1790s as the **Ship**. When the Wye Bridge was re-opened in 1816 the pub was renamed the **Bridge** and a few years later the:

> messuage, tenement or dwelling house with the brewhouse and outbuildings near the Bridge and called the Bridge Inn occupied in the past by William Badman

was leased from George Waters, Yeoman, to William Badam, Victualler. A further deed of 1839 records William Ivins taking over the tenancy from

An outing from the Bridge Inn in 1928

The Bridge Inn in 1983

Thomas Waters of the inn 'fronting the River Wye and a Malthouse now forming a court of five houses'. Further tenants followed before Whitbread acquired the premises in the 20th century

In 1983 Whitbread were selling the **Bridge** for £65,000, but the landlord, who had been the licensee for fifteen years, reported to the *South Wales Argus* that 'There was no way he would pay £65,000 for the place, he regretted having to leave'. A few months later the *Argus* reported 'Ancient pub gets a costly facelift ... in another step towards the redevelopment of the lower end of the town' a £25,000 development programme was planned by the new owners

Above: The Bridge Inn in 2006. Below: The inn sign in 2001

who felt that 'lower Chepstow is undergoing an important redevelopment. It is no longer suffering from the planning blight which it has in the past. This area should provide a lovely location.' Since then the pub has been stripped of its Whitbread sign and now serves Bass, Worthington and Hancock's ales.

From Bridge Street, the present day St. Ann Street leads in an easterly direction to meet Lower Church Road. In the 19th century St. Ann Street was called St. Anne's Lane, and was where a number of licensed premises were situated. The **Lord Wellington** had been established by 1830, when William Jenkins was the publican, until it closed sometime after 1858. The **Sailors Tavern** seems to have been a large old inn recorded in 1820 as a 'messuage, tenement or dwelling house together with garden thereunto adjoining and belonging, situate in said town of Chepstow in tenure of Elizabeth Phillips and commonly called the Sailor's Tavern'. Previous tenants included John Wickham, Elizabeth Waters, Katherine Gillum, Thomas Chapman, Andrew Phillips and George Chapman.

The **Sailors Tavern** was kept by John Harris in 1830 and Seth Jones in 1835. It may have been renamed the **Wyelands** which then became the **Old England Tavern** as recorded in deeds of 1847:

> All that messuage or mansion house formerly called the Wyelands but now called or known by the name of the Wyelands with the gardens, greenhouse, plant, pleasure grounds' yards' stables, coach house and outhouses.

The **Old England** was kept by John Hatton in 1849, but it must have closed shortly after this date.

FULLY - LICENSED PROPERTY,

Freehold Free from Tithe and Land Tax,

KNOWN AS THE

"OLD WYE HOUSE,"

Occupying a corner situation between St. Anne's Lane and The "Back," Chepstow.

It is Brick-built with Slated Roof, and contains

BAR, TAP ROOM, SMOKE ROOM with Private Entrance, LARGE BACK KITCHEN, PANTRY, W.C., and on Two Floors above are TEN BED ROOMS and BOX ROOM. Under the Bar is CAPITAL CELLAR.

The above premises are let to Messrs. ROGERS & Co., on a Yearly Michaelmas Tenancy at a Rent of **£19 10s.** a year.

Sale of the Old Wye House in 1899

In St. Ann Street the former **Wye House** is the only property recognisable as an inn, standing prominently on the corner adjoining buildings that were once used as a wine store by the Chepstow Wine and Spirit Co. in the mid-19th century. The **Wye House** existed as a licensed premises in 1828 and in 1830 was kept by Thomas Hayton followed by Peter Brown and then

Wye House wine store 2006

William James, who ran the pub from at least 1849 to the 1880s. About this date it was leased to Messrs. Rogers and Co., who were still the tenants when the Duke of Beaufort sold the **Old Wye House** in 1899. A few years after the sale the **Old Wye House** closed.

St. Ann Street leads on to The Back which curves around and along the bank of the river Wye where much activity would have taken place during the 18th, 19th and early 20th centuries. Since then the area has been dramatically transformed from an important port to a pleasant riverside with a green, band-stand, seats and a pedestrian pathway. With help from the Chepstow Society's *Chepstow Riverside Trail* this interesting site can be explored from Brunel's Tubular Suspension Bridge of 1852/3 at the eastern end to the road bridge of 1816. Along the way, the Town Slip, the Dry Dock, the Packet Slip, the Gloucester Hole and the Gunstock Wharf can be identified with guidance from the *Trail* and the informative plaques. Beyond the Tubular Bridge at the Meads was the site of National Shipyard Number 1 towards the end of the First World War, and the site where tank landing craft and sections of Mulberry Harbour were constructed during the Second World War.

William Coxe in 1801 wrote:

> In 1792, the shipping belonging to this place amounted to 2,800 tons, and in 1799 was increased to 3,500. ... The principal exports are timber, of which a thousand loads per month have been occasionally shipped for the dock yards, large quantities of grain for the Bristol market, and the different manufactures of the country, namely, pig, wrought and bar iron, wire, tin plates, coal, tar, grind and mill stones, paper and cider. Oak bark likewise is a considerable article of export, and is usually shipped from hence to Ireland; the average annual quantity cannot be estimated at less than 6,000 tons; but from peculiar circumstances in 1799 it exceeded 9,000.

Charles Heath, a few years later, added:

> A considerable trade is here carried on with Bristol, South Wales and Ireland, particularly in the timber and bark line, quantities which are annu-ally shipped to those places, as the yards, wharfs and houses testify.

He also wrote about the ship building industry being supplied with timber from the Forest of Dean, Monmouth and Herefordshire to build 'ships of war, frigates, sloops, transports or victualling vessels'.

With all this shipping industry taking place at The Back, it is not surprising to discover that there was a large number of inns, pubs and beer houses offering refreshment, lodgings and a meeting place for the workers, bargees and merchants. In 1835 there were six named pubs and two unnamed beer-houses, but with several name changes in the 19th century it is a diffi-cult task to trace individual pub's histories. Over a decade later there were at least ten licensed premises there, a number that gradually decreased to the present one and only pub that survives in The Back.

Entering The Back from St. Ann Street, the first noticeable pub site is a property called Lord Nelson House, which started as the **Mermaid** before 1806 when William Partridge, victualler, occupied:

> All that messuage for many years since used as a tenement a dwelling house now a public house commonly called or known by the name or sign of the Mermaid with the several outbuildings, yards and premises thereto adjoining.

The deed also mentions an adjoining 'small tenement' and gives a good description of The Back at that date. The **Mermaid** was:

> lying and being in or near the back in the said town of Chepstow and are bounded on or towards the South East by a warehouse or cellar belonging to the said Warren Jane and the waste lands belonging to the Duke of Beaufort on the South West by the street or way leading from the land of the Dry Dock towards the Slip on the North West by the road or way between the said premises and the said Dry Dock and on or towards the North East by a new warehouse and premises belonging to the said Warren Jane.

William Partridge was still the occupier of the **Mermaid** in 1810 before its name was changed to the **Lord Nelson**, presumably to commemorate the admiral. There was a long succession of different publicans at the inn throughout the 19th century, and at the start of the 20th century Richard Cumper, the licensee, was summonsed for persistent cruelty to his wife. The *Chepstow Weekly Advertiser* of 15 June 1901 recorded the hearing of 'A Chepstow Publican and his Wife'. He had given his wife dozens of black eyes and, although he was licensee of the **Lord Nelson**, he was a boiler maker by trade, but preferred to go fishing. He had called her a 'drunken harlot and everything that was bad. Last Wednesday he knocked her about, cut her lip, and banged her head against the dresser'. From the detailed account it appears that Annie Cumper was always drunk according to her husband, but he appeared a worthless sort of landlord.

The **Lord Nelson** survived this scandal and was kept by William Pates in 1923 and William George in 1937 probably about the date that the Stroud Brewery acquired the inn. It was taken over by West Country Breweries in 1962 and finally closed in 1968. The premises in 1982 looked empty and

---

CHEPSTOW—THE LORD NELSON INN.

ALL THAT messuage or Inn at The Bach Chepstow known as The Lord Nelson Inn with the cottage and the outbuildings and land thereto adjoining and belonging.

The 1937 sale of the Lord Nelson

The Lord Nelson in 1982

Right and above: The renovated Lord Nelson House in 2006

derelict, but fortunately by 2006 the property had been renovated with a clear sign Lord Nelson House.

Along this inner part of The Back was the **Hole in the Wall**, which featured in the *South Wales Argus* in 1963 when a photograph of the old inn was discovered by a reader. This rare 1905 photograph showed the inn before it closed in 1908. Apparently it had opened in 1822 and was once owned by the Duke of Beaufort; its customers being 'mainly sawyers and shipwrights who worked along the banks of the Wye'. Records show that the inn was established at a date in the late 18th century, and that Luke Mitchell was the

The Hole in the Wall in 1906

publican in 1830 followed by the Lewis family until the end of the 19th century. After its closure the **Hole in the Wall** was demolished and the site redeveloped.

Four other licensed premises, which were only open for a few years at the Back, were the **Prince Regent**, kept by Jemima Thomas in 1830, the **New Zealand**, kept by James Stacey in 1849, the **Cooper's Arms**, kept by John Prickett in 1849 and the **Steam Packet**, kept by John Davis in 1830. The **Prince Regent** was named after the son of George III, who became Prince Regent in 1811. All of these inns appear

An early painting of the Hole in the Wall Inn

The site of the Steam Packet

to have closed before 1850, although the **Steam Packet** may have become the **Packet Quay** beer-house of 1859 run by Elizabeth Lewis before she took over the **Victoria** in Lower Church Street. The **Steam Packet** was probably named after the 'Bristol and Chepstow Steam Packet' known as the *Wye* which conveyed passengers, luggage, horses and carriages between the two towns.

At an earlier date another type of boat was sailing down the Wye, conveying early tourists from Ross to Chepstow as described by Hughes and Hurley:

> From around the mid-eighteenth century the untamed and virtually unknown beauty of the river Wye attracted the attention of poets, writers, artists and gentlemen of taste seeking the Picturesque ... A boat trip was taken from Ross which became known as the *Wye Tour* with its origins attributed to the Rev. John Egerton'. This Rector of Ross started a boat trip for his wealthy friends that became a fashion and was commercialised by boatmen and innkeepers along the Wye. Heath noted in 1828 that the price of a boat from Ross to Chepstow was 'three guineas;- beside provisions for the Boatman; which may be allowed for, or found by the company, as is most agreeable to the party.

It is hard to imagine the fashionable society of the past alighting from boats at Chepstow due to the tide and the extremely muddy and steep banks at the Riverside.

One inn which may have catered for these tourists is the present day **Boat**, originally known as the **Chepstow Boat** in 1789, which stood on the edge of the former Dry Dock.. In 1849 Phillip Fisher was the innkeeper, probably the Fisher recorded by Farr in *Chepstow Ships* as the master of a sloop called the *Chepstow* in the 1830s and '40s. Richard Cumper from the **Lord Nelson**, even with his history of misbehaviour managed to take on the tenancy of the **Chepstow Boat** when it was offered for sale in 1899.

As part of the Duke of Beaufort's estate for sale in 1899, the **Chepstow Boat** was advertised as 'The Fully Licensed Freehold Riverside Inn' with 'Large Warehouse Adjoining. Occupying an important Corner Position on the

Back facing the River Wye and Packet Slip'. The inn contained a tiled entrance porch, bar, parlour, sitting room, kitchen, pantry, cellar and a paved yard, and there were three bedrooms on the first floor and two attics. It was suggested that the large warehouse of two floors could be used to extend the premises.

Other landlords followed, including William Joy and Joe Ellis during the early 20th century. Ann Rainsbury in her book on Chepstow wrote about Joe Ellis who also worked as a boilerman, salmon fisher and horse trainer. He also ran a steam launch for tourists between 1906 and 1923 during his time as landlord of the inn. Some time before 1937 the **Chepstow Boat** became unlicensed even though Arnold Perrett and Co. owned the property. They sold a parcel of land at the Back together with the former inn and its outbuildings in 1937 to the Cheltenham Original Brewery.

CHEPSTOW.—THE BOAT INN.

ALL THAT piece or parcel of land comprising Two thousand one hundred square feet or thereabouts situate at the corner of the "Back" and facing the River Wye and Packet Slip in the town of Chepstow in the County of Monmouth TOGETHER with the messuage or tenement erected thereon and known as the Chepstow Boat (the license for which has now been discontinued) and the warehouse thereto adjoining and all outbuildings and appurtenances thereunto belonging.

The 1937 sale of the one-time Chepstow Boat

The Boat Inn in 1982

The **Chepstow Boat** remained closed, and in 1982 it was in a sad state. It was eventually sold and in 1984 the *South Wales Argus* reported that 'An old riverside inn at Chepstow which is currently being renovated was provisionally granted a drinks licence by Chepstow licensing magistrates'. The court had been told that 'the inn had been de-licensed for a considerable number of years and was in an isolated spot on the river bank', and that it 'had been allowed to get a little bit seedy and the conversion of the inn would help enhance the area'. The new licensees added that 'they intended to have a bar

The Boat Inn in 2006

Left: The author's husband in the Boat. Right: Stained glass enhances the name

with an eating area and would cater for adult customers and said the area was becoming popular with tourists and hoped the move would encourage the council to tidy up the river bank'.

The **Boat** was certainly worth saving as an inn – it was sympathetically restored into an attractive building from the exterior, and the former ware-

A 1982 photograph of the Salutation which became the Wye Knot

Left: The Chartist plaque on the Wye Knot
Right: The Wye Knot in 2006

house has been cleverly incorporated into the pub allowing plenty of room for diners. The original pub has retained some features of the past which provides a cosy atmosphere. In 2006 CAMRA recommended the **Boat** as 'A welcoming riverside pub with a genuine nautical air to it. Worth the search' with John Smith's Bitter, Wadworth's 6X and Guest Ales in the summer which included Gem from Bath and Wye Valley from Herefordshire.

The Back continues up river to the **Wye Knot** in a splendid position overlooking the Wye and the Green. It was a restaurant, which has been refurbished and is now called **Petrus**. In a restaurant guide of 2007 it is described as 'A 16th-century riverside restaurant run in a relaxed and friendly manner' with 'a daily-changing blackboard menu and invariably includes some of the more local dishes'. The **Wye Knot** was originally the **Salutation** in the early 19th century, being renamed the **Lord John Russell** around the mid-1840s until it closed a few years later. The **Lord John Russell** was a sign taken from the English statesman, a reformer who named the Liberal Party, and the innkeeper may have been a supporter. On the outside of the **Wye Knot** is a blue plaque erected by the Chepstow Society which reads:

> The Chartists. From this riverside on 3rd February 1840, John Frost, William Jones and Zephaniah Williams, the convicted leaders of the Chartist March on Newport, sailed to begin their transportation to Van Diemen's Land (Tasmania).

The **King's Arms** at The Back was yet another pub recorded by Ivor Waters.

Sources and References

General Works
Improvement by Sea and Land, Andrew Yarranton, 1698
The Torrington Diaries, Hon. J. Byng, 1781-87
The Book of Trades, 1811
Paterson's Roads, E. Mogg, 1828
The Great Western Railway, P.R. Gale, 1926
The Old Roads of South Herefordshire, H. Hurley, second edn. 2007
Ancient Dean, B. Walters, 1992
The Ross and Monmouth Railway, M. & C. Glover, 1994
Bridges on the River Wye, A. Crow, 1995
The Rivers Wye and Lugg Navigation, V.R. Stockinger, 1996
The Ross, Monmouth and Pontypool Road Line, S.C. Jenkins, 2002

Journals, Newspapers etc.
Gloucester Journal
Hereford Journal
Hereford Times
Monmouth Beacon
Monmouth Merlin
Chepstow Weekly Advertiser
Newscuttings file at Chepstow Library
Monmouthshire Directories, 1822-1937
Monmouth Road Act, 1755
Licenses, 1822-1835, 1858
Deeds, Documents, Sale Particulars, Gwent Record Office
Documents and Manuscripts, Monmouth Museum

Maps
Millerd, 1686
Cadell & Davies, 1800
Plan of Monmouth, 1835
Ordnance Surveys, 1887, 1903, 1918, 1998
Street Atlas, 2004, 2006

The County

An Historical Tour in Monmouthshire, W. Coxe, 1801
Excursion Down the Wye, C. Heath, 1828
Banks of the Wye, R. Taylor, c1860
A History of Monmouthshire, Sir J. Bradney, v. 1 & 2, 1904-1913
Wye Valley, E.J. Burrow, 1905
The Registers of Chepstow Parish, W.H. James, 1913
Chepstow and Tintern Guide, 1926
Wye Valley Guide, 1946
Chepstow Ships, G. Farr, 1954
Wye Valley Industrial History, P. Harris, 1968
Monmouth, K. Kissack, 1975
Chepstow Historic Walled Port, c.1977
The Port of Chepstow, I. Waters, 1977
The River Wye, K. Kissack, 1978
Parish of Penalt, c.1980
Exploring Gwent, C. Barber, 1984
Turnpike Roads, I. Waters, 1985
Fedw Villages, R. Howell, 1985
Victorian Monmouth, K. Kissack, c.1985
Penalt, Penalt P.C., 1987
Nelson and the Hamiltons on Tour, E. Gill, 1987
Monmouth and the River Wye, A. Helme, 1989
Chepstow and the River Wye, A. Rainsbury, 1989
Tales of Old St. Arvans, J. Edmonds, 1990
Wye Valley Guide, 1990
Tinterns' Story, J. Russill, c.1990
Llandogo, Village of 1000 Steps, Trellech Council, 1990
The Green Dragon Archaeological Evaluation, Monmouth Archaeology, 1998
Water Powered Industries of the Lower Wye, S.D. Coates, 1992
Chepstow Riverside Trail, Chepstow Society, 1993
The Wye Valley Walk, H. & J.. Hurley, 1994
Monnow Bridge and Gate, M.L.J. Rowlands, 1994
The Lordship, Parish and Borough of Monmouth, K. Kissack, 1996
The Folklore of Monmouthshire, R. Palmer, 1998
Chepstow Town Trail, 1998
The George and the Gate, Chepstow Society, 1999
The Buildings of Wales; Gwent, N. Pevsner, 2000
Trellech 2000, J. Wimpenny, 2000
The Tintern Trail, Forestry Commission, 2002
Monmouth and its Buildings, K. Kissack, 2003
Chepstow Town Trail, Chepstow Society, 2003
Llandogo Village Walks, Monmouthshire C.C., 2003
Poetry Bands in Paving, Chepstow Town Council, 2005
Chepstow High Street Regeneration Scheme, Chepstow Town Council, 2005

Whitebrook, Whitebrook Conservation Group, 2005
Chepstow Castle, R. Turner & A. Johnson, 2006
The Priory and Parish Church of St. Mary Chepstow, nd

Inns, Breweries, Cider and Wine
Inns, Ales and Drinking Customs, F. Hackwood, *c.*1904
Wintle's Brewery Properties, 1929
Arnold Perrett & Co. Sale, 1937
Wintle's Brewery Sale, 1937
Drink, A Simon, 1948
Alton Court Brewery Sale, 1962
Stroud Brewery Sale, 1962
British Inn Signs, E. Delderfield, 1965
Inns and Taverns of Chepstow, I. Waters, 1976
The Inns and Friendly Societies of Monmouth, E. Davies & K. Kissack, 1981
The English Inn, J. Burke, 1981
Pub Names, L. Dunkling & G. Wright, 1987
Brewing Industry, L. Richmond & A. Turton, 1990
Anglo-Saxon Food and Drink, A. Hagan, 1995
Paths and Pubs of the Wye Valley, H. & J. Hurley, 1998
The Pubs of Ross and South Herefordshire, H. Hurley, 2001
The Pubs of the Royal Forest of Dean, H. Hurley, 2004
A Matter of Taste, J. Hurley, 2005
The Eating Out Guide, 2005
The Pubs of Hay and the Golden Valley, J. Eisel & F. Bennett, 2005

Index

243